THE TOTAL CLASSICAL GUITARIST

MARTHA MASTERS

edited by
Nathaniel Gunod

Alfred Music Publishing Co., Inc.
P.O. Box 10003
Van Nuys, CA 91410-0003
alfred.com

ISBN-10: 0-7390-8931-5 (Book & CD)
ISBN-13: 978-0-7390-8931-6 (Book & CD)

CD recorded and mastered by Ryan Ayers at Sunburst Recording Studios, Culver City, CA

Cover Photos
Inset: © dreamstime / alenavalad • Guitar: by Richard Bruné

Interior Photos by Scott Kugler
Photo of Dynarette cushion on page 18 courtesy of Guitar Salon International, www.guitarsalon.com
Photo of adjustar on page 18 courtesy of Kirkpatrick Guitar Studio, www.kirkpatrickguitar.com
Photo of classical guitar strap on page 18 courtesy of Levy's Leathers Ltd., www.levysleathers.com

Contents

0
Track 1

A compact disc is available with this book. Using the disc will help make learning more enjoyable and the information more meaningful. Listening to the CD will help you correctly interpret the rhythms and feel of each example. The symbol to the left appears next to each piece or example that is performed on the CD. Example numbers are above the symbol. The track number below each symbol corresponds directly to the piece or example you want to hear. Track 1 will help you tune to this CD.

About the Author

The *Illinois Times* wrote that guitarist Martha Masters "is on a swift and certain trajectory to star territory." Masters' playing has been described as "seductive" (*Fort Worth Star-Telegram*), "intelligent and natural" (*Guitar Review*), and "refined and elegant" (*American Record Guide*). She has received critical acclaim as a solo recitalist, as a chamber musician, and as a soloist with orchestras. Recent concert seasons have included performances on concert series and at festivals in China, England, Denmark, Spain, Poland, Serbia, Italy, Germany, Paraguay, Peru, Puerto Rico, Canada, Mexico, and throughout the United States.

Masters has released five recordings on the Naxos and GSP labels and authored a critically-acclaimed technique and repertoire book for intermediate and advanced classical guitarists, *Reaching the Next Level*, published by Mel Bay.

In October of 2000, Martha Masters won first prize in the Guitar Foundation of America (GFA) International Solo Competition, which included a recording contract with Naxos, a concert video with Mel Bay, and an extensive North American concert tour. In November of 2000, she also won the Andrés Segovia International Guitar Competition in Linares, Spain and was a finalist in the Alexandre Tansman International Competition of Musical Personalities in Lodz, Poland. Prior to 2000, Masters was a prizewinner or finalist in numerous other international competitions, including the 1999 International Guitar Competition "Paco Santiago Marín" in Granada, Spain, the 1998 Tokyo International Guitar Competition, and the 1997 GFA International Solo Competition.

In addition to being on the guitar faculty at Loyola Marymount University in Los Angeles, Masters is also the President of the Guitar Foundation of America (GFA), dedicated to supporting the instrument, its players, and its music in the US and throughout the world.

Masters received both the bachelor and master of music degrees from the Peabody Conservatory, where she studied with Manuel Barrueco, and completed the doctor of musical arts degree at the University of Southern California as a student of Scott Tennant.

Acknowledgements

Special thanks to Burgess Speed and Nat Gunod for their expertise and guidance throughout the process of writing this book.

Introduction

Welcome to *The Total Classical Guitarist!*

The guitar is one of the most popular instruments on the planet, played by tens of millions of people around the world. The classical guitar boasts much smaller numbers. In fact, many people don't really know what "classical guitar" is, or that it even exists! The simple fact that you've picked up this book puts you ahead of the crowd.

The classical guitar and its repertoire as we know it today came to life in the 19th century. There were many predecessors to the guitar, with a wide variety of constructions, that were used primarily to accompany singing or other instruments. Composers of the late classical and early romantic era were the first to write music for the classical guitar as we know it today, and the first to treat it as a concert instrument rather than a supporting or folk instrument. The guitar of that time was a bit smaller than what is used today. It utilized gut strings but sounded similar to today's classical guitars. It was during the late classical and early romantic era that technical standards and repertoire for the instrument began to develop. The first virtuoso soloists also emerged during this time, including Fernando Sor, Mauro Giuliani, and many others, the majority of whom were both performers and composers.

The classical guitar has continued on its path over the past two centuries, with the biggest turning point being the life and career of Andrés Segovia. It wasn't until Segovia arrived on the scene in the early 20th century that non-guitarist composers began to write for the instrument, contributing serious works to the repertoire and earning respect for the instrument in concert halls around the world. Were it not for the influence that Segovia wielded, the classical guitar might still be just a parlor instrument, with a handful of virtuosos scattered around the world.

Segovia gave credibility to the guitar as a serious classical instrument, capable of delivering the same technical and musical range as other respected classical instruments. Since that time, the pedagogy for the classical guitar has been codified, non-guitarist composers dare (on a regular basis) to write for the instrument, university and conservatory programs have expanded to include classical guitar as one of their instruments, and the level of playing has skyrocketed.

The technique required to play the classical guitar is fundamental to all styles of playing and will serve you well, regardless of your end goals in music. To get the most out of this book, you should have a bit of knowledge and experience playing some kind of guitar. Though the fundamentals will be reviewed, the primary focus will be on skills needed by players coming from different musical backgrounds (for instance, rock or blues). If you have never played guitar of any type, you will find the pace to be a bit fast. Take extra time with all the exercises and pieces, and seek out additional repertoire to support your development before moving on to chapters with more challenging techniques. Pieces have been arranged according to their level of difficulty within each chapter. So, if you're struggling, work on pieces that came earlier in the chapter and skip the later ones until you've gained more confidence and experience.

There are a few fundamental differences between playing classical guitar and playing guitar in other styles. First is the importance of reading music. Many non-classical players have successful careers without ever learning to read, but this is unlikely in the world of classical music. Being a skilled reader opens many doors to you, so put in the time—it's worth your effort. Sitting position and right-hand technique are also quite different for classical guitar—the good news is they can be applied to other styles of playing and will help you improve in these styles.

Many of the greatest acoustic and rock guitarists have roots in classical study. The techniques learned in studying the classical guitar can lead to amazing playing in all styles. One of the hardest things to do is to change the way you play. It's much easier to learn a new skill than to change a habit that you've had for a long time. I encourage you to take the time and apply all the technical advice given in this book. Don't expect changes overnight, but do the work with great diligence, and you'll be amazed with the results.

Good luck, and enjoy!

Chapter 1: Getting Started

Purchasing a Guitar

One of the best favors you can do for yourself when learning classical guitar is to get a respectable nylon-string instrument that is set up to help you succeed. Poorly made guitars make it difficult to play and difficult to produce a good sound, both of which will lead to frustration and loss of interest.

A good guitar doesn't need to cost a fortune. Of course, quality often does (and should) improve with increase in cost—but if you're just testing the waters in the world of classical guitar, you can still get a decent student instrument at an affordable price. Following are a few considerations as you search for the right guitar:

1. **How do your left-hand fingers feel on the strings?** Guitarists familiar with other styles know what is meant by the term *action*, which refers to the height of the strings from the fingerboard. The action on a classical guitar is a bit higher than on an electric guitar, so you should anticipate working a bit harder with the left hand. However, it shouldn't be dramatically different as you go up the neck—it should increase gradually, like a bunny slope, not like a black diamond ski slope. If it feels too difficult to play in the upper positions, find another guitar.

2. **What is the quality of the sound?** If the strings are making a buzzing sound, there's a chance the action is too low. This can often be fixed, but be sure to address this issue before buying an instrument. If you have a more sophisticated ear (and a higher budget), you can start getting into tonal considerations: Is it too bright, or too muddy? Does it project well enough? Generally, at the lower end of the price spectrum, it is enough to look for a guitar that is set up well, and, as you approach the middle-range instruments, you can get more particular about the finer points of a guitar's tone.

3. **Check the intonation.** *Intonation* refers to the pitch accuracy of an instrument. This is a huge consideration, not to be underestimated, because if there's a problem, it's often not easily corrected. A good way to check the intonation is to play an open string, then play the harmonic (see page 93) on the same string at the 12th fret. They should sound exactly one *octave* apart. (An octave is the distance in pitch between 12 frets on the guitar.) If it's out of tune, it could be a bad string (which is fairly common) or a bad guitar. You can also check by comparing the open string to the fretted note at the 12th fret, but you must take care not to bend the string at all, as this can affect the pitch. If, when using this procedure, you have one string that is out of tune and the other five are in tune, then, most likely, you just have a bad string. But if three of your strings are out of tune at the 12th fret, the intonation is bad and you should probably look for a different guitar. Constantly struggling to get a guitar in tune will drive a good musician crazy—and an inexperienced musician even crazier! You need all the help you can get when learning something new.

The Importance of a Good Teacher

The next best thing you can do for yourself is find a good teacher. There is no substitute for having someone check your progress every week. Not only does it provide great motivation, but a live teacher can give you instantaneous feedback on anything you are doing right or wrong. This feedback, based on your personal strengths and weaknesses, will help you improve as quickly and efficiently as possible. And improvement is the key to motivation and success. Pick the right teacher and your money will be well spent—guaranteed.

Parts of the Guitar

To the right is a diagram of a classical guitar, with all its parts labeled.

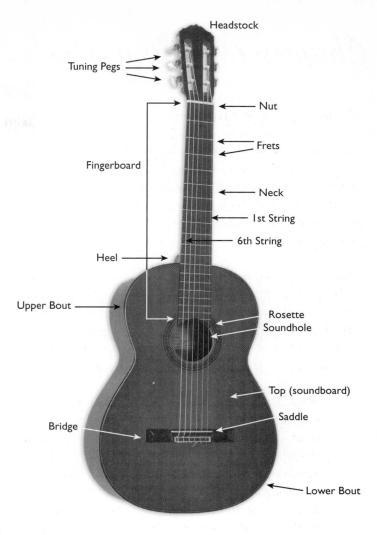

Headstock

Tuning Pegs

Nut

Frets

Fingerboard

Neck

1st String

6th String

Heel

Upper Bout

Rosette
Soundhole

Top (soundboard)

Bridge

Saddle

Lower Bout

Identifying the Fingers

The fingers of the left hand are numbered 1–4, starting with the index finger (see below).

The right-hand fingers are indicated using abbreviations of their Spanish names (see below).

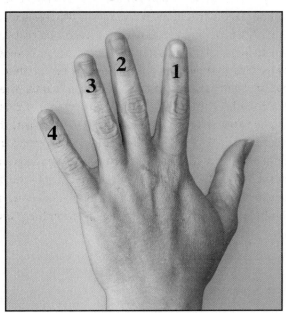

The left-hand fingers.

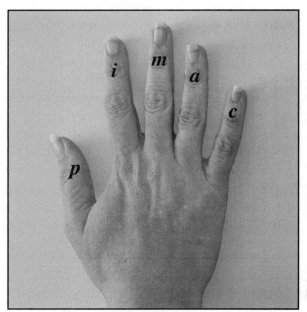

The right-hand fingers.

p =	*pulgar.*	Thumb.
i =	*indicio.*	Index finger.
m =	*medio.*	Middle finger.
a =	*anular.*	Ring finger.
c =	*chiquita.*	Pinky.

Tuning

Most guitarists today have electronic tuners. Even professionals (in all styles) frequently take their tuners onstage to increase the accuracy of their tuning and to reduce the downtime between pieces. However, all guitarists should learn to tune by ear. Electronic tuners are a great way to make sure you're tuning correctly, but you need to develop your musical ear so that you can distinguish between being in or out tune without the aid of an external device. You can do this using the method of *relative tuning*.

Relative Tuning

Relative tuning is a method in which the guitar is tuned relative to itself, matching the pitch of each open string (except the 6th string) to the pitch of a fretted note on the adjacent lower string. Before learning how to do this, let's look at a diagram of the fingerboard labeled with string names and numbers (see below).

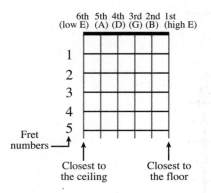

Okay, let's start.

1. First, you need to tune your 6th or 5th string to a reference, or starting, pitch. You can do this with an electronic tuner, but make sure to turn it off and adjust the other five strings using relative tuning. If you don't have an electronic tuner, you can get a reference pitch from an electronic *metronome*. (Most metronomes, which are adjustable time-keeping devices, can generate an A440 tuning note.) You can also use a keyboard, tuning fork, or Track 1 of the accompanying CD.

2. Let's assume you tuned the 6th string (low E) to a reference pitch and it is in tune. Now, you need to tune the 5th string to the 6th. The open 5th string is an A note, and that same pitch can be produced on the 6th string by fretting the 5th fret. (Note: proper right-hand technique is covered on page 19, and left-hand technique, page 27.) Play the A on the 6th string, then compare that to the open 5th string. They are supposed to sound the same. If they do not, determine whether the 5th string is too high or too low, then adjust the corresponding tuning peg until the open 5th string matches the A on the 6th string. If the pitch is too low, turn the tuning peg to make the string tighter; if the pitch is too high, turn the tuning peg to loosen the string. At this point, the bottom two strings are in tune.

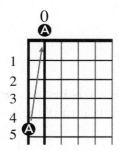

3. Our next step is to tune the 4th string using the 5th string as reference. The pitch of the open 4th string is D, and we can produce that same pitch on the 5th string at the 5th fret. Make any necessary adjustments to the 4th string.

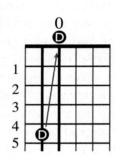

4. Next, tune the open 3rd string to the 5th fret of the 4th string.

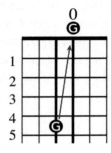

5. Now, tune the 2nd string to the 3rd. At this point, we deviate from the established pattern. The open 2nd-string B note can be produced on the 3rd string—not at the 5th fret, but at the 4th.

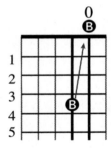

6. For the last string, we're back to our pattern, matching the open 1st-string E to the E on the 2nd string at the 5th fret.

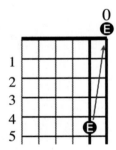

Once you're done, check a couple of chords (if you know any) to make sure everything sounds in tune. Some instruments require that we make some "compromises" in our tuning, though hopefully you picked a great instrument that has good basic intonation, especially in the lower positions.

Learning to tune can be frustrating, and it is easy to just rely on the tuner. However, you are encouraged to tune by ear every day and use the tuner (or Track 1 of the accompanying CD) to check your tuning. You'll develop a better ear this way, and this will make you a better musician.

Chapter 2: Practice Strategies

A Note for Crossover Players

Learning the guitar as a beginning student is a challenging task. Learning the classical guitar when your background is in another style of guitar playing may or may not be much easier, depending on the habits you have developed and that are ingrained in your technique.

The best advice (though this won't work for everyone) is to go "cold turkey" on any other styles of playing, at least for a short period of time. This is the quickest way to develop and strengthen new techniques and skills. For some people, this isn't possible—you may have a band that depends on you or some other valid reason. In any case, if you cannot devote yourself exclusively to the classical style for the first eight weeks or so, make sure to follow this advice:

1. If, in your study of classical guitar, you are trying to make adjustments in your left-hand technique, you must apply these adjustments to your other styles as well.

2. If you're making adjustments to your right hand and wrist position, those changes can and should be applied to your other styles of playing.

3. If you realize you have tension in your shoulders, you should address this issue not only when playing classical but when playing all styles of guitar.

Continuing to play other styles with your old technical habits will delay or prohibit the improvements necessary to progress through the pieces in this book. All of these changes will greatly improve not only your classical playing, but any other styles as well.

The Classical Aesthetic

One of the biggest challenges facing crossover guitarists (or anyone exploring classical music for the first time) is the difference in aesthetics. Many popular styles are based primarily on chordal motion. When players with this background come to the classical guitar, one particular challenge they face is learning to connect melodies smoothly across chord changes that are being fingered simultaneously. This part of phrasing is an innate part of classical technique on any instrument, but may require a change of perspective for a crossover player.

Similarly, players who come from mostly a strumming background probably haven't focused on tone production to the extent necessary for playing classical guitar. Tone production is important on any instrument and in any style, but in classical music, an extremely high value is placed on it. So again, it's going to require a change in perspective for a crossover player to appreciate the importance of spending hours refining their contact point (see page 20), analyzing the movement of their fingers, and changing the position of their wrist to achieve the "perfect" tone.

Finally, the guitar is a relatively unforgiving instrument. We're fortunate to have frets that allow us to achieve precise intonation (which a bowed string player must achieve without the aid of frets). However, frets may cause extra headaches in terms of playing cleanly. The classical aesthetic is certainly a "clean" one, so it's important to avoid buzzing sounds by placing your fretting finger in the sweet spot just behind (to the left of) the fret. Of course, most styles value playing cleanly, but the transparency of much classical music makes this all the more important. So, another change in perspective is necessary to appreciate the incredible level of refinement and detail required to become a convincing classical player.

Making the Most of Your Practice Time

There are some things you can do going forward to maximize your practice time while learning to play the classical guitar.

1. **Apply your new classical technique to other styles you may be playing.** Prolonging old habits only delays (or prevents) the adoption of newer, better habits.

2. **Don't move on to the next concept in this book until you've mastered the one at hand.** When you do move on, be sure to review regularly so as not to lose grip on the material already covered.

3. **Practice basic technical exercises in front of a mirror.** This allows you to check your technique from a more objective viewpoint. In fact, you should do as much of your technical practice as possible while watching your hands, either in the mirror or directly.

4. **No mindless practice!** This is not only a waste of time, but can be damaging. You're guaranteed to revert to old habits if you're playing without engaging your brain.

5. **Record yourself periodically, to get a reality check.** Hearing a playback can bring a little clarity to your self-perception.

6. **Set goals.** If you're not progressing as you'd like, analyze the situation. Are you putting in enough practice time? If not, do you need to practice more—or adjust your expectations? Are you missing something in your technique? Reaching milestones will motivate you to continue on your path to success.

PHOTO COURTESY OF ANTONIO MIR MARQUÉS

*It wasn't until **Andrés Segovia** arrived on the scene in the early 20th century that non-guitarist composers began to write for the instrument, contributing serious works to the repertoire and earning respect for the instrument in concert halls around the world. Were it not for the influence that Segovia wielded, the classical guitar might still be just a parlor instrument, with a handful of virtuosos scattered around the world.*

Chapter 3: Reading Music

Reading music is seen as a requirement for most musicians; however, many very accomplished guitarists have famously (or infamously) achieved acclaim without ever having mastered this skill. Yes, it is possible to play the guitar without reading standard notation, but your options are so much greater when you've gained music literacy! It's not as hard as one may think. In this chapter, we're going to review the basics. If this material is entirely new to you, be sure to spend lots of time here before moving on. Students new to reading have often expressed frustration quickly, saying, "I can't do it!" Don't give up. There is no secret to reading music. You simply need to memorize the basic elements: how to identify notes on the staff and where to find them on the guitar. There is no way around it. If you feel the process is going too slowly for you, treat it more academically. How would you study for a Spanish vocabulary quiz? How would you memorize a speech you have to recite? There is work involved, and you must do it. The good news is, once you put in the work, it pays dividends in your musical life.

The Staff

Music is written on a *staff* consisting of five lines and four spaces.

All guitar music is notated in *treble clef* 𝄞, and you'll see that symbol at the beginning of every line of music. (Note: Treble clef is also called G clef because its curl surrounds the G line on the staff.)

Most written music is divided into *measures*, which are separated by *barlines*. A *double barline* indicates the end of a section or piece, and a *final barline* indicates the end of a piece.

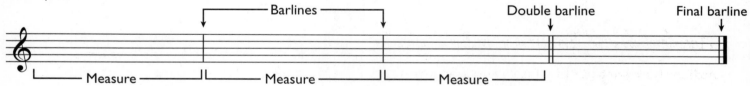

If a composer wants to indicate that a section of the music should be repeated, this will be indicated with a *repeat sign*.

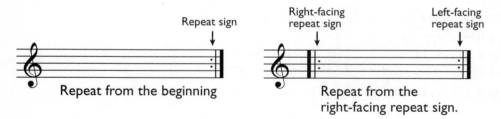

Reading Pitches

The *musical alphabet* consists of seven letters that repeat: A–B–C–D–E–F–G, A–B–C, etc. The staff works like a ladder, with each line and space representing a different letter of the musical alphabet. Even if you only remember one note name and its corresponding location on the staff, you can, in theory, figure out any other note by simply counting lines and spaces and moving through the musical alphabet one letter at a time.

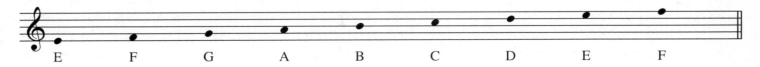

| E | F | G | A | B | C | D | E | F |

Learning which line or space corresponds to each note is simply a matter of committing this information to memory. There are a couple of mnemonic tricks you can use to speed up the learning process. The spaces of the staff spell "FACE." The lines of the staff don't spell any particular word, but many people use the sentence "Every Good Boy Does Fine" as a memory aid—the first letter of each word in the sentence represents one line of the staff.

Space Notes   Line Notes

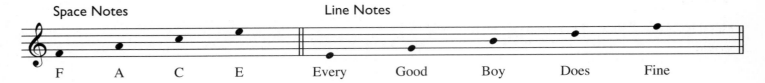

| F | A | C | E | Every | Good | Boy | Does | Fine |

The staff can be extended in either direction using *ledger lines* to accommodate notes that are higher or lower than those on the staff. These lines (and the spaces in between) function as additional rungs on the ladder, and the corresponding note names can be determined by counting through the musical alphabet in the same manner as with the staff. Learning to read notes on ledger lines may be more challenging at first, but these too will become familiar with time.

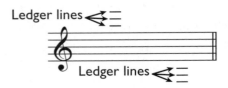

Accidentals and Enharmonic Equivalents

Accidentals are symbols that raise, lower, or return a note to its original pitch, and their effect lasts through the remainder of the measure in which they appear. A *sharp* (♯) raises a note by a *half step* (one fret). A *flat* (♭) lowers a note by a half step. A *natural* (♮) restores a note to its original pitch within the key (see page 15).

The notes that lie between the *natural notes* (the notes of the musical alphabet: A–G) can be referred to using either sharps or flats, depending on the nature of the piece. When notes are "spelled" differently but have the same pitch (such as G♯ and A♭), they are referred to as *enharmonic equivalents.* (See right.)

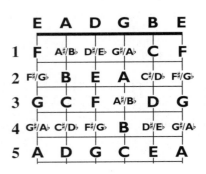

Notice there are no accidental notes between B–C and E–F. The interval between these sets of notes is a half step. The interval between all other natural notes is a *whole step* (two frets). For example: C–C♯ = half step; C♯–D = half step; C–D = whole step.

The Logic of the Fingerboard

On the guitar, the distance from one fret to the next (or from an open string to the 1st fret) is a half step. To figure out options for playing any note in a higher position, you must become familiar with the entire fingerboard. Learning *1st position* (the first four frets and the open strings) is a great starting point, but you'll want to go beyond that in order to develop a full understanding of the instrument and its possibilities. Move slowly and methodically as you memorize the location of notes on the staff and on the fingerboard. You can try exercises like playing a scale on one string (shifting up and back, as opposed to crossing strings). Of course this is not musical, but it forces an understanding of the structure of scales as well as an understanding of how the fingerboard works. The better you know the fingerboard and the staff, the better reader you'll be.

Complete Guide to the Fingerboard

Following is a guide to the notes on the fingerboard. This information does not need to be memorized before moving on. Learning the fingerboard is a process, and this chart is provided for your reference only.

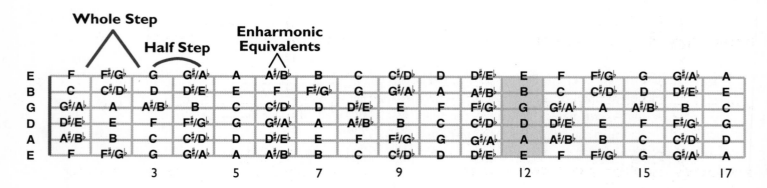

Keys and Key Signatures

A *key* is the tonal center of a piece of music. Each key is based on the major or minor scale from which it gets its name. For instance: the key of C Major is based on the notes of the C Major scale, the key of A Minor is based on the A Minor scale, etc.

A *key signature*, which appears at the beginning of every line of music and tells us what key the music is in, indicates which notes are to be altered throughout the piece. These alterations occur regardless of the octave in which these notes appear (unless otherwise indicated). There are seven flat keys and seven sharp keys (plus the *relative keys**). Below is a chart showing all the possible key signatures.

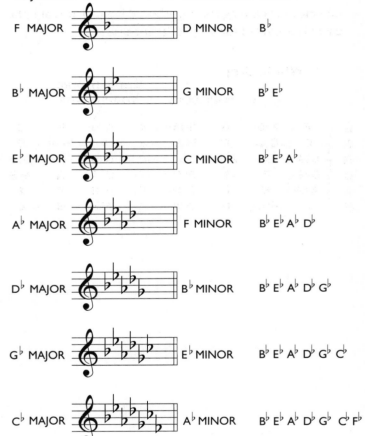

* Relative keys are major and minor keys that share the same key signature, for instance, G Major and E Minor (both keys have one sharp, F#).

Rhythm

Rhythm is the organization of music in time and involves how notes are counted. Notes are counted in reference to a *beat*, which is a division of musical time that can be thought of as the pulse of the music (for example: 1, 2, 3, 4; 1, 2, 3, 4, etc.).

Note Values

The duration of a note is referred to as its *value*. Following are the basic note values we'll deal with in this book.

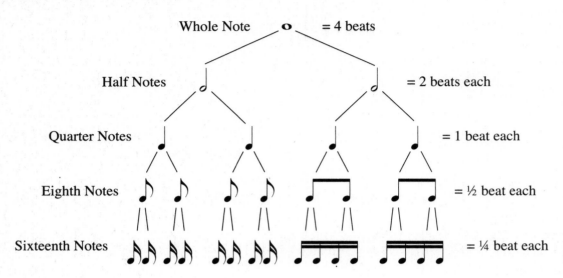

Rest Values

A *rest* is a symbol indicating silence in music. Each note value above has a corresponding rest value.

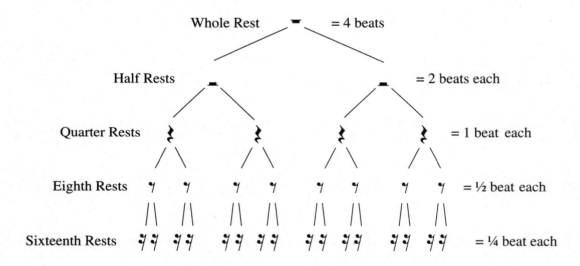

Dotted Notes

If a *dot* appears to the immediate right of any of the notes or rests above, it adds half of the original value to itself. For example: A half note normally lasts for two beats. Half of two is one. Two plus one equals three. Therefore, a dotted half note lasts for three beats.

Dotted half note (𝅗𝅥.) = 3 beats

$$2 + 1 = 3$$

Dotted quarter note (♩.) = 1 ½ beats

$$1 + \tfrac{1}{2} = 1\tfrac{1}{2}$$

Dotted eighth note (♪.) = ¾ of a beat

$$\tfrac{1}{2} + \tfrac{1}{4} = \tfrac{3}{4}$$

Time Signatures

The note values given above represent the way these notes are counted the vast majority of the time (exceptions to this will be introduced shortly). However, these basic note values work in tandem with *time signatures* that tell us how many beats are in each measure and which note value gets one beat. The time signature, which consists of one number above another, appears at the beginning of each piece.

$\frac{4}{4}$ = 4 beats per measure
Quarter note ♩ = one beat

As you can see above, the top number tells us how many beats are in each measure, and the bottom number indicates which note receives one beat. So, in $\frac{4}{4}$ (pronounced "four four") time, there are four beats in each measure, with the quarter note receiving one beat. In time signatures that have a "4" on the bottom, the quarter note is the basic unit of time used for counting through the measures.

Complete measures of $\frac{4}{4}$ could look like any of the following (among many other possibilities).

Count: 1   2   3   4   1   2   3   4   1   2   3   4   1   2   3   4

As you can see in the example above, measures of $\frac{4}{4}$ are counted: 1, 2, 3, 4; 1, 2, 3, 4, etc.

$\frac{4}{4}$ is such a common time signature that it is referred to as *common time* and is often indicated with a $\mathbf{C}$ at the beginning of the piece.

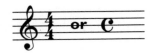

Now, for the tricky part. When the bottom number of a time signature is "8," the eighth note is the basic unit of counting. When the bottom number is "2," the half note is the basic unit. In these cases, all other note values are adjusted relative to this count. So, for example, let's compare the values of the notes in $\frac{3}{4}$ versus $\frac{3}{8}$ and $\frac{3}{2}$. (See chart to the right.)

If the composer chooses a shorter note value for the bottom number in a time signature ($\frac{3}{8}$), they are indicating a faster *tempo* (speed) for the piece. If a longer note value is chosen ($\frac{3}{2}$), a slower tempo is indicated.

	$\frac{3}{4}$	$\frac{3}{8}$	$\frac{3}{2}$
Whole note			2
Half note	2		1
Quarter note	1	2	½
Eighth note	½	1	¼
Sixteenth note	¼	½	⅛

Chapter 4: Sitting and Right-Hand Position

Sitting Position

Establishing a correct, but comfortable, sitting position is crucial to your success on the classical guitar. Those coming from other styles might find the classical sitting position a bit awkward. Remember, everything new and different feels uncomfortable at first—you will need to spend some significant time in the new position before you know what really works for you. So, approach this with patience and an open mind.

There are two factors to consider when determining your sitting position:

1. Be sure that your body is relaxed and that you aren't using it in a way that could cause long-term fatigue or damage.

2. You need to position yourself in a way that allows you to do all required of you in terms of playing technique.

When playing classical guitar, it is necessary for the guitar neck to be at approximately a 45-degree angle. Some players hold it slightly higher, which can work as well. But much lower than that, and you won't be able to comfortably reach all the notes in the upper position—nor will you be able to fret multiple strings without having dead notes. Though many popular-style guitarists hold the neck nearly parallel to the ground, you'll notice, if you look at the strongest players in any genre, most of them elevate the neck in one manner or another. This angle provides the best access to every part of the fingerboard.

← Footstool

Correct sitting position.

Footstools and Other Devices

To achieve this sitting position, most classical guitarists use a footstool under their left foot, as seen in the photo above. However, some players who have problems with back pain elect to use an alternate guitar support device, of which there are many on the market (see photos below).

These devices usually attach to the underside of the guitar to prop it up on the left thigh, allowing both feet to remain flat on the floor while still elevating the neck of the guitar. Either option achieves the desired position, which is what really matters.

Adjustar.

Dynarette cushion.

Classical guitar strap.

Basic Right-Hand Position

Right-hand technique is the area requiring the most work for many crossover guitarists. It is central to producing a good tone, to playing cleanly, and to the development of speed and endurance. The hand must be positioned in a way that allows the fingers to work with minimal tension (that's the speed and endurance part of the equation), to be consistent (that's the accuracy part), and to be in the sweet spot for the contact point with the string (that's a large part of what determines your tone).

Let's start with the basic approach and setup of the hand.

1. Keep all your joints in the middle of their range of motion—nothing bent too far one way or the other.

2. The wrist should be basically straight, not bent left or right, up or down (see photos below). This is a common problem for many acoustic guitar players, who develop the habit of collapsing the wrist so that it sometimes even touches the top of the guitar. This just won't work for classical playing. The good news is that if you fix your technique here, it will make you a stronger player in other styles as well.

3. Be particular about the part of your arm making contact with the guitar. Your forearm (not your bicep), just slightly below your elbow, should be in contact with the guitar.

4. Watch out for where the arm comes to rest on the guitar. Many players tend to position the arm too low. Your forearm should rest more or less in line with the bridge.

5. Pluck near the bottom of the soundhole for the standard "normal" sound. (Keep in mind, however, that everyone will have a slightly different home base for their right hand.)

Arm rests in alignment with bridge

Keep wrist straight

Pluck near the bottom of the soundhole for the standard "normal" sound.

Wrist bent too far to the right.

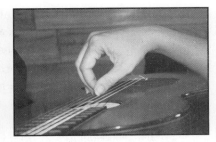

Wrist up too high.

Wrist bent too far to the left.

Wrist too low.

Wrist with appropriate height.

Contact Point and Fingernails

Most classical guitarists use the fingernails of their right hand in combination with the flesh of the fingertips as "picks." This produces a clearer, louder tone than would be possible with flesh alone.

If you're a crossover player who is devoted to playing other styles, it may be impossible for you to maintain fingernails.

An option for acoustic players, whose fingernails tend to get chewed up on the steel strings, is to use acrylic nails, which are tough enough to withstand steel strings while still providing a good tone on the classical guitar. If you're not able to maintain fingernails, the best thing you can do is keep the nails very short and out of the way—nothing sounds worse than catching a string on an unshaped nail!

Contact Point

The *contact point* is where the right-hand finger meets the string when plucking. A good contact point is critical to a consistently good tone. The desired contact point is where the nail and flesh meet on the left side of the finger.

Contact point for the thumb.

Contact points for the fingers.

Fingernail Shape

Your nails should be shaped in a bit of a ramp, so the string can just slide off the nail without catching on any corners. The exact length of the nail varies from player to player. Generally speaking, shorter nails move through the string more easily—but the shorter the nail, the more precise you need to be with your contact point. This is a balancing act, and each player needs to work this out for him/herself, preferably in consultation with an experienced player.

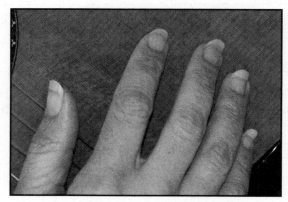

Your fingernails should be in the shape of a ramp.

Fingernail Maintenance

After your nails are the right shape, you need to become conscientious about their maintenance. Filing them with an emery board won't suffice. Good tone production requires you to polish the edges of your nail (the top edge, the front edge, and the bottom edge—any part that will come into contact with a string) with very fine polishing paper. Any tiny scratches in your nail will be heard as you pull through the string, and your sound won't have the focus and power it could with the right attention to nail care.

There are nail buffers out there that have a very fine grade polishing paper, but you can't rely on the buffers you may find at a grocery store; these may or may not work, and you won't know until you're home and the package is open. Many don't have polishing surfaces fine enough, and they won't accomplish your goal.

Look for nail buffers designed for guitarists; or buy "wet or dry" sandpaper (1000 grade) to put the polishing touches on your nails. Don't underestimate the importance of this step. It may take a bit of effort to find the right product, but once you have it, it will make a big difference in your sound.

Finally, be sure to buff your nails with this fine-grade paper every time you sit down to play guitar. If you practice twice in one day, buff before each session. Every time you step away from the guitar, you encounter little things in life that leave tiny scratches on your nails. Don't accept those tiny scratches as part of your sound. Approach the guitar every time with your nails in great shape.

Free Stroke

The basic and most common stroke in classical playing is the *free stroke*. Keeping the hand still and letting the finger do all the work, follow these steps:

1. Position your right arm so that the large knuckle joints (see photo at far right for the locations of all the finger joints) are more or less over the top of the strings you're plucking.

2. Pluck the string with the finger and follow through toward the palm of the hand.

3. Empty the tension from your finger and allow it to return to its starting point without touching any other strings.

If your knuckle joints are too far behind the strings, you'll either have a very limited follow-through (which affects your speed and tone production) or you'll constantly bump into the string adjacent to the one you intend to pluck. So, be sure to keep your wrist straight and your knuckle joints positioned correctly.

Try the following exercise. Use free strokes alternating between the *i* and *m* fingers. Use the rests to prepare the next finger on the string at its correct contact point.

Free stroke preparation.

Free stroke execution.

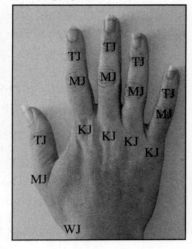

The finger joints.

TJ = tip joint
MJ = middle joint
KJ = knuckle joint
WJ = wrist joint

Rest Stroke

Another type of stroke is the *rest stroke*. As above, keep your hand still and let the finger do all the work while following these steps:

1. Position the right arm so that the knuckle joints are a couple of strings behind whatever string you are plucking.

2. Pluck the string with the finger, following through and coming to rest on the next lower string with the fingertip.

3. Empty the tension from your finger and allow it to return to its starting point.

4. Be sure to keep the hand still and let the finger do all the work.

Rest strokes tend to be a bit louder and fuller sounding than free strokes. However, they have their limitations, as they prohibit the ringing of neighboring strings. In any case, it is important to learn both types of strokes and not to rely too heavily on one or the other.

Try the free-stroke example above, this time using rest strokes.

Rest stroke preparation.

Rest stroke execution.

Note: When working with the right hand, make sure your fingers and thumb do all the work. The right hand should never bounce as you pluck the string. Playing with a moving hand is like playing darts while running at the board. You'll be a lot less accurate in finding the right strings with a bouncy hand!

Playing with the Thumb

Let's look at proper thumb technique. The motion for the thumb should originate where the thumb joins the wrist, and the contact point is where the nail and flesh meet on the left side of the thumb.

Here is a simple exercise where you will switch back and forth between two strings, performing rest strokes with the thumb. Keeping the hand still and letting the thumb do all the work, follow these steps:

1. Plant your fingers on the first three strings (*a* on the 1st string, *m* on the 2nd, and *i* on the 3rd)—this will serve as an anchor for the hand.

2. Plant the thumb on the 6th string at the correct contact point described above.

3. Pull through the string (toward the floor) and come to rest on the 5th string, immediately emptying the tension from your thumb. Your goal is to arrive on the string in the perfect contact point, ready to make the next stroke on the 5th string. If you didn't quite arrive in perfect position, make the necessary adjustment.

4. Pluck the 5th string, coming to rest on the 4th string.

5. Return your thumb to the starting point on the 6th string and repeat.

While performing the exercise described above (and notated below), be careful to define your contact point precisely. Ultimately, you should be landing in exactly the same spot with each stroke, ready to play the next note without readjusting. This will take practice! Don't give up. This technique is essential for achieving clarity in your thumb tone and has a direct impact on how well you're able to project the bass notes of a piece. Let's try the exercise.

After you're comfortable with the above exercise using rest strokes, try it with free strokes. Instead of following through and coming to rest on the next string, follow through to the tip joint of the *i* finger with a slight upward motion to clear the next string. Then, empty the tension in the thumb and return to its starting point. Because of the free-stroke motion, your hand will lose a bit of its stability and control—so, practice diligently until you can land in the same spot every time.

Alternating Fingers on a Single String

Now that you're comfortable using the thumb, it's time to use your fingers. Generally speaking, when using the fingers, we alternate between *i* and *m*. There are plenty of exceptions to this; for example, arpeggios (see page 25) and more complex passages featuring intermittent use of the *a* finger. But *i*–*m* alternation is by far the most common use of the fingers.

Let's start with the rest stroke.

1. Place your thumb on the 4th or 5th string (wherever it is comfortable) as an anchor.

2. Place your *i* finger on the 1st string, with the knuckle joints approximately over the 3rd string (rest-stroke position). Check your wrist to be sure that it is basically straight and not overly arched or collapsed.

3. With your *i* finger resting on its precise contact point, pull through the string and come to rest on the 2nd string. When you've completed the stroke, immediately empty the tension from your *i* finger.

4. Prepare your *m* finger on the 1st string in its precise contact point, then pull through the string, coming to rest on the 2nd string.

5. Release the tension from your *m* finger.

6. Repeat this process over and over, slowly—paying particular attention to the precise contact points, the follow through to the 2nd string, and the immediate release of tension.

Now, try the exercise.

When you are comfortable using rest strokes on the exercise above, try it with free strokes. To position your knuckle joints over the top of the 1st string, you'll need to slide your arm just slightly forward. Do a few test strokes without worrying about alternating or where to place the next finger; just focus on your follow-through. Following through is the most critical part of having great tone and projection, not to mention staying relaxed in order to eventually gain speed.

Be sure the entire finger is moving—not just the lower portion. Really watch the top part of the finger to make sure it is moving in toward the palm and not up toward the ceiling.

Crossing Strings

Once you are comfortable with free strokes and rest strokes on a single string, you're ready to try crossing strings. This is a skill that is frequently underestimated in its importance and its degree of difficulty. In order to maintain your wrist position and your relative alignment with the strings, it is necessary to make slight adjustments in the position of your arm as you cross the strings.

There are two fundamental ways to cross strings, and many players use a hybrid technique, combining these two approaches.

Approach 1

One way to cross strings is to roll forward or backward, using the flesh on the underside of the forearm as a sliding fulcrum. You never lose contact between your arm and the instrument, but use the "play" in your flesh to create the small movement necessary to cross strings. If you choose this method, be careful not to unintentionally change your wrist position, adding too much arch (as you move to lower strings) or flattening out too much (as you move to upper strings).

Approach 2

Some players prefer to leave the point of contact truly fixed, and instead of rolling forward and backward using the flesh, they move the arm at an angle as they cross the strings (imagine a record needle, something moving from a fixed point—in this case, your elbow).

Depending on the musical circumstance, either of the two methods above will work. Just be clear of your intention before you move.

Alternating and Crossing

As you experiment with alternating fingers and crossing strings, you'll notice it is much easier to cross to higher strings with the *m* finger and to lower strings with *i*. This has to do with how our hands work naturally, allowing for minimal hand movement in the crossing. Don't fight it! Work out your fingerings in a way that utilize this natural tendency whenever possible. However, there are many situations in which you'll need to perform the less natural string crossing as well, so be sure to practice both ways. Keep in mind that the less natural way requires more arm movement.

Try the following exercises, experimenting with different string crossings. The way they are fingered here represents the "natural" way to cross strings, but you should also practice these exercises starting on the opposite finger. (Note: Example B is in $\frac{3}{4}$ time, which has three beats per measure with the quarter note getting one beat. $\frac{3}{4}$ time is counted 1, 2, 3; 1, 2, 3, etc. Example C is in $\frac{2}{4}$ time, which has two beats per measure with the quarter note getting one beat. $\frac{2}{4}$ time is counted 1, 2; 1, 2, etc.)

Arpeggios

An *arpeggio* consists of the notes of a chord played separately, one after the other, rather than simultaneously. Most acoustic players are familiar with arpeggios. However, even if you've played arpeggios in other styles, it's important to re-examine your technique in order to play them in the classical style.

The key to great arpeggios is having great right-hand technique. The more relaxed you are, the faster you'll be able to play them; the more stable your hand is, the more accurate you'll be; and the more consistent you are with your contact points, the better your tone and projection will be. So, as you begin to work with arpeggios, keep those fundamentals of technique firmly in your mind.

Before you start playing anything, including arpeggios, check the following:

1. Sitting position

2. Right hand/arm setup

3. Contact points

Before playing the first note of any exercise or piece (including those in this book), make sure all three of the above items are exactly as they should be. Then, immediately upon finishing the piece, check these items again. If you managed to maintain your position, great! If not, start doing checks part way through the exercises so you remain conscious of these technical points as you're practicing.

Arpeggio exercises are included at the end of each of the remaining chapters. We'll start with relatively easy examples that will increase in difficulty as the book progresses. It is important to incorporate arpeggios into your daily practice routine. Just be sure you're practicing them for quality and not simply to check them off your list of things to do for the day. Make sure to analyze your technique while you practice arpeggios; otherwise, you'll just be reinforcing your current level of playing, not improving.

The following arpeggios should be practiced "fully prepared," meaning the right-hand fingers will be in their contact points before beginning each arpeggio pattern. Use the rests to allow yourself a quick check of your contact points. Making sure your fingers are in the right place will lead to better tone and projection.

The following exercise is written with three fingering possibilities:

1. Strict right-hand alternation. This is not the most efficient way to play this exercise, but it is great practice in string crossing.

2. In the second fingering, the thumb should play rest strokes on the first two notes (thereby preparing for the subsequent note) and free strokes on the remaining notes. This should be played as a fully prepared arpeggio: the right-hand fingers are in place on the strings before beginning the exercise. This is the most common and fluent way to play an arpeggio passage like this.

3. A "standard" arpeggio, where *i* and *m* will re-extend to play more notes following the *a* finger. In the first sequence of *p*, *i*, *m*, and *a*, the fingers will all be in place on the strings, but the *i* and *m* used for the last two notes will not have much preparation time. This is the most advanced of the fingering options, though again, not necessarily the best way to finger such a passage—consider it a good technical exercise.

Julian Bream (b. 1933) is an English classical guitarist and lutenist who made his professional debut at the age of 14. One of the most important classical guitarists of the 20th century, he broadened the repertoire for the instrument and played a major role in the revival of Elizabethan music.

Chapter 5: The Left Hand

Basic Position

The demands of classical guitar repertoire require that we be very precise with the use of the left hand. There are several things you should look for when setting up your left-hand position:

1. **Generally, the inside of your palm should be parallel with the neck of the guitar.** There will, of course, be exceptions to this. For example: When you simultaneously play two notes on two strings at the same fret, you'll be required to rotate the hand into a position that is no longer parallel. However, the vast majority of the time, you should aim to remain parallel with the neck. This allows easier access to the notes on the lower strings with your 3rd and 4th fingers and will be a contributing factor in your ability to play with speed and accuracy—two goals that speak to all of us!

2. **Position your thumb midway behind the neck, halfway between the 1st and 6th strings.** (See Fig. 1 below.) Your thumb acts as an anchor, balancing your fingers as they do their work. For that reason, your thumb should be positioned between the 1st and 4th fingers. Many guitarists tend to play with the thumb too far to the left, which puts the 4th finger (already the weakest finger) at a disadvantage. When in 1st position, the thumb should be, approximately, behind the 2nd fret. As you shift, the thumb should always remain one fret higher than whatever position you're in (as we'll cover in depth in a future chapter).

3. **Fret the strings with your fingertips, not with the pads of your fingers.** This allows you to clear the next string and to cleanly play more than one note at a time. In addition, be sure to place your fingertips just to the left of the fret for the cleanest tone and most efficient use of strength. (See Fig. 2 below.)

4. **Your fingers should not stick together—they should all function independently.** When playing in 1st position, the fingers generally hover over their "assigned" frets: 1st finger over the 1st fret, 2nd finger over the 2nd fret, 3rd finger over the 3rd fret, and 4th finger over the 4th fret. It may take a bit of training to get the fingers in the hovering position, but it pays off when the time comes to play notes quickly. Fingers that lump together don't function independently, which means you will not be able to develop the necessary speed.

5. **Your wrist should, as with the right hand, be basically straight.** It should not bend left or right, or be overly arched or collapsed. As you shift up and down the neck, your left-hand position should remain the same. This is a big challenge for many people. Make sure that when you shift, your thumb is moving with you—this defines the position you're in and whether or not you'll be able to reach the necessary notes while maintaining good technique.

6. **Your left elbow should be wherever it needs to be to support the wrist and general position requirements mentioned above.** The entire arm will move as you shift up and down the neck. Avoid holding the elbow out too far and the opposite problem of pinning it to your side. Let it hang naturally. Be flexible, and base your elbow position on where it needs to be to support the wrist and hand. Your elbow is at their service.

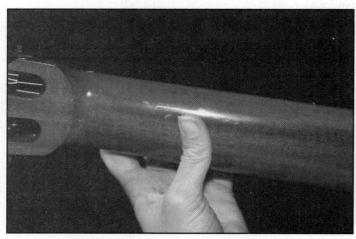

Fig. 1: Correct thumb position.

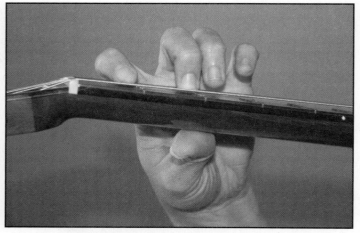

Fig. 2: Fret the notes with your fingertips, just to the left of the frets.

Efficient Use of Hands

In playing any instrument, efficiency of motion is critical to being a great player. You want to make the most of all your motions, not exhausting yourself (and taking yourself out of position) with bigger movements than required. When playing classical guitar, the left hand tends to make the most serious errors in this regard.

A note of warning is that some players take this concept too far and limit their motions in a way that involves excessive tension. As you apply the instructions in this section, be sure that all motions are relaxed. Tense, compact movements will get you nowhere!

The efficiency we're talking about here ultimately relates to your awareness of the movements that need to be made—and your ability to slow those movements down and gain control over your fingers. For example, when changing from a G7 chord to a C chord, the move is actually quite small: the fingers remain in approximately the same formation but are moved to different strings (see below).

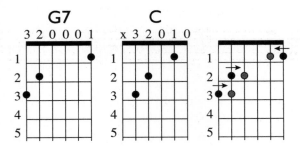

If you're changing from a B7 to an E chord, the 2nd finger stays in place, the 1st finger stays at the same fret but moves over one string, the 3rd finger stays at the same fret but moves over one string, and the 4th finger is lifted from the fingerboard.

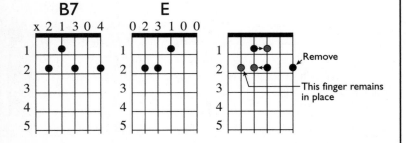

If your fingers release entirely from the first chord in either of the above scenarios—without thought for the fingering of the target chord—you'll move considerably farther and expend more energy than is necessary to complete the change. This results in slow chord changes.

If you play other styles of guitar, you've likely already worked out the issues described on this page. Now, you must take these same principles and apply them to what may seem like more complex moves while reading classical music. In reality, the moves often aren't more complex—they are just less familiar to you.

Learning an instrument is faster when you engage your brain, as opposed to just doing things over and over (though repetition has its place as well). Be conscious of what fingers the chords have in common, the exact distance each finger must travel, whether or not a shift is involved, etc. Have a solid understanding of what is required of the left hand and then make the move as efficiently as possible. The more you stay aware of these considerations while learning a piece—as opposed to going back and fixing bad habits later—the quicker and more enjoyable the process will be for you.

Chromatic Scales

A great way to practice proper left-hand position and efficiency is to play *chromatic scales*. A *scale* is a series of consecutive notes in a particular order, and the term *chromatic* means movement in half steps. So, a chromatic scale is a series of notes arranged in half-step movements.

Always remember: Before you play each exercise, check your right-hand setup, then your left-hand setup, and then begin. When you're done, check both hands again to see if you kept them in their correct positions.

Let's start with a simple chromatic scale on the 1st string in 1st position.

Now, try crossing strings. Play the following chromatic scale (skipping open strings for now, to make it an easier pattern), starting on the 3rd string and crossing up to the 1st string—still without shifting position.

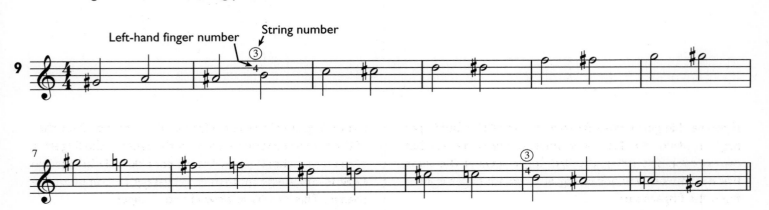

Now, for a bigger right-hand string crossing: a chromatic scale (again skipping open strings) in 1st position, covering all six strings.

In the beginning, chromatic scales are great for learning and practicing basic technique because you don't have to worry about what note comes next; you are reading, but you are also aware that the next note is on the next fret. Now, the challenge is to start integrating your reading skills with the use of both hands.

Chapter 6: Integrating Reading Skills with Right- and Left-Hand Technique

As you work through the pieces in this chapter, pay special attention to your right- and left-hand technique, as well as reading the notes and rhythms correctly. This takes practice, but be patient. With time, it will all feel very natural.

Ode to Joy

Following is the melody for "Ode to Joy" by Ludwig van Beethoven (1770–1827). When practicing this piece, be mindful of your technique in both hands and pay attention to the following tips.

Practice Notes

1. Play this piece as slowly as necessary to play it accurately. Hesitating before playing a note is preferable to playing the wrong note. Hesitations can be worked out in the long run, while correcting wrong notes can be more difficult to deal with.

2. It's up to you whether you want to start with rest strokes or free strokes. However, once you're comfortable with the content of the piece, switch to the other stroke to ensure development of both types. And whichever stroke you are using, be sure to consistently alternate between the *i* and *m* fingers.

3. Left-hand fingerings are not included so that you don't become reliant on reading the fingerings instead of the notes themselves. In general, if it is a 1st-fret note, play it with your 1st finger; if it is a 2nd-fret note, play it with your 2nd finger, and so forth.

4. Be calm and mentally ready for each note before you play it.

5. Watch out for the dotted notes in measures 4, 8, and 16—and pay attention to the counting numbers underneath those measures.

Ode to Joy

Ludwig van Beethoven

Count: 1   2 & 3   4

1   2 & 3   4

1   2 & 3   4

* This is a metronome marking, indicating that this piece is to be played at a tempo of 80 quarter-note beats
   per minute. These markings will be used throughout the book.

Song of the Toreador

For ease of reading, the following melody appears in here $\frac{4}{4}$ time, though Georges Bizet (1838–1875) originally wrote it in $\frac{2}{4}$. As covered on page 17, composers can use time signatures to indicate the feel of a piece. $\frac{2}{4}$ generally signifies a faster tempo, and, in this case, creates a march-like feel. However, at this point, just keep it slow and focus on your technique.

Practice Notes

1. In measures 9–10, 15–16, 17–18, and 19–20, you'll notice *ties*, which are curved lines (⌒) joining two notes of the same pitch that last for the combined value of both notes. In other words, pluck the first note and let it ring out for the duration of both notes.

2. Pay careful attention to the key signature. This piece has three sharps, which means it is in the key of A Major. Be sure to sharp every instance of the notes F, C, and G; and watch out for the additional sharps in measure 14.

3. Even though you have to reach the 4th fret for the F♯ in measure 7 and the G♯ in measure 15, be sure to stay in 1st position. We haven't covered position shifting yet, so it's best to keep your left hand in one place.

Track 5 *Song of the Toreador*

Georges Bizet

Asturias (Leyenda)

Following is the main melody from one of the most popular pieces for classical guitar. Composed by Isaac Albéniz (1860–1909), it is presented here in a simplified form to help you focus on thumb technique.

Practice Notes

1. Start by using either free strokes or rest strokes. When you are comfortable with the content of the piece, switch to the other stroke.

2. Pay careful attention to your contact points and create a strong, full sound with your thumb. If you're interested in someday playing the full version of this piece, focus on the fundamentals now. Then, when you start working on the complete version, it won't seem as intimidating.

3. The $\frac{6}{4}$ time signature tells us there are six beats in each measure and the quarter note gets one beat. This isn't the most common time signature, but it's easy enough to count (1, 2, 3, 4, 5, 6; 1, 2, 3, 4, 5, 6, etc.).

4. The end of this piece features our first attempt at reading and playing a *chord* (something we'll get more into in the next chapter). A chord consists of three or more notes played simultaneously. When notes are to be played at the same time, they are stacked on top of each other on the staff. Place the fingers of your left hand one note at a time, from bottom to top: E–B–E–G#–B–E. Once your fingers are in place, you may recognize this as an E Major chord. Now, sweep your right-hand thumb downward across the strings in a light rest-stroke motion— moving smoothly through the strings one at a time. This should be a controlled motion across all six strings creating the impression of a chord spread gently, not individual notes played in succession. This sweep across the strings, or *roll*, is referred to as *quasi arpi* and is indicated with the symbol.

Track 6 Asturias (Leyenda)

Isaac Albéniz

♩ = 84

Note: Make sure you have a good grip on the preceding exercises and concepts before moving on to the slightly longer pieces that follow. Don't be in a rush! The more quality time you spend building up your technique, the better off you'll be when you tackle the more challenging pieces in this book.

Etude in C

"Etude in C" was written by guitarist/composer Fernando Sor (~1778–1839). Really take your time when working through this one!

Practice Notes

1. Strings 1–3 are known as the *treble* strings ("treble" meaning high in pitch), and strings 4–6 are the *bass* strings ("bass" meaning low in pitch). This piece moves between the bass and treble strings (with the exception of the 1st), requiring you to alternate between the right-hand thumb and fingers for a smooth, seamless sound. Some notes will feel most natural when played with the thumb, and the remaining notes should generally alternate between the *i* and *m* fingers.

2. Pay attention to balancing *dynamics* (how loudly or softly you play) and tone production as you switch between the thumb and fingers across the various strings.

3. As with most of the demanding pieces in this book, use free stroke throughout. It's great to practice rest stroke in your scales and other exercises, but for compositions that move around a lot, free stroke is the best option. As you advance, you'll find ways to incorporate rest strokes for emphasis and musical effect.

4. Be sure to keep your left hand in 1st position. We'll move away from this eventually, but for now, staying in 1st position will help develop good left-hand technique and muscle memory for finding notes.

5. This piece includes *repeat signs.* If you see a left-facing repeat sign only :||, go back to the beginning and play again. If you see a left-facing repeat sign preceded by a right-facing repeat sign ||:, go back to the right-facing repeat sign and play again.

Track 7

Etude in C

Fernando Sor

Etude in C Minor

Here is another piece by Sor.

Practice Notes

1. Notice the key signature for C Minor has three flats: B♭, E♭, and A♭. This means that all B, E, and A notes (in any octave) are to be played flat unless otherwise marked. If you have trouble remembering the flats, don't hesitate to pencil them in. Your ability to remember will improve with time, and it's better not to perpetuate bad habits by playing wrong notes.

2. As with the previous piece, your left-hand should be in 1st position. The only exception to this is in measure 9: Since the note preceding measure 9 is fretted with the 3rd finger, use your 4th finger to fret the G (a 3rd-fret note) on the *downbeat* (first beat) of measure 9. This will help you avoid a break in the melody as your finger leaves one note to prepare for the next.

3. "Etude in C Minor" is in $\frac{3}{4}$ time (1, 2, 3; 1, 2, 3, etc.) but begins with a single quarter note before the first barline. This is called a *pickup note*, and it leads into the downbeat of the first full measure. By using a pickup, a piece can begin on a beat other than 1. In addition, when a pickup note is used, the last measure of the piece will account for the remaining "missing" beats to complete a full measure in the given time signature; this is called an *incomplete measure*. To start this piece, count beats 1 and 2 silently, and then begin on beat 3.

Fernando Sor (~1778–1839) was a Spanish classical guitarist and composer, who, to his contemporaries, was considered the best guitarist in the world. Although he composed for many other instruments, he is best known for his works for classical guitar. His Twenty Studies for the Guitar, as edited by Andrés Segovia, is a staple of classical guitar pedagogy.

Etude in C Minor

Fernando Sor

♩ = 80

Etude in A Minor

This piece by Dionisio Aguado (1784–1849) is a great arpeggio study.

Practice Notes

1. So far, you have played only fully-prepared arpeggios, with all fingers touching the strings before each pattern began. For this piece (and for normal arpeggio technique), you'll advance to *sequential planting*. This approach has you touch each finger to the string right before plucking it. When using this technique, be sure you feel the contact point—as opposed to "swiping" at the string—before playing each note. Make every stroke full of intention, and you'll develop strong, rich-sounding arpeggios.

2. The left hand moves through simple chord shapes that, if you have some experience on the guitar, you may be familiar with. However, watch out for some less common fingering indications, designed to help you connect the *voices* (see Practice Note 3 below) more smoothly as you change from one chord to the next.

3. This is the first piece that features two distinct *voices*, or musical parts. Each voice must independently fulfill the time signature in each measure (in this piece, which is in $\frac{2}{4}$, there are 2 beats per voice per measure). The voices may (and often do) move independently of one another. Different voices are often distinguished by stem direction; stems point upward in the top voice and downward in the bottom voice. Before trying to understand the composite rhythm, count out each voice separately to ensure you have a solid grasp on how each line works individually. (Note: In this piece, this concept may be a little difficult to understand because the two voices feature some identical notes. For example, the first note of the piece, A, has a stem going up and a stem going down. Though this note is considered part of both voices, you only play a single A note. For a clearer visualization of the concept of voices, see Example 17 on page 42.)

4. This piece is to be played *legato*, or with a smooth, connected sound. This is an important aspect of classical guitar playing. Not all classical music is legato, but if you're not intentionally (for musical reasons) breaking a line, you should be able to achieve this flowing sound. In this piece, the legato feel is achieved by holding each chord shape and letting the notes ring out for as long as possible before changing to the next.

5. Note that the time signature for this piece is $\frac{2}{4}$ (two beats per measure with the quarter note getting one beat).

Etude in A Minor

Track 9

Dionisio Aguado

Technical Supplements

Technical practice should always have a purpose beyond checking it off your list for the day. Mindlessly running through scales is a waste of time, not to mention boring! Be sure you always have a goal when practicing these exercises. At first, if you're new to reading music, your goal might simply be to read the notes correctly. Once you get comfortable with the notation, your goals can shift to addressing technical issues, generally focusing on one challenge at a time.

Start by focusing on your right hand and whatever issues need to be addressed there (hand position, follow-through, tone production, etc.). Then, move on to left-hand issues (keeping your palm parallel to the neck, playing with your fingertips, etc.).

If you find it too difficult to focus on technique while doing these exercises, then go back and work more with the open-string arpeggios and string-crossing exercises in the earlier chapter. There's no shame in going back—it's about getting the material right. Many professionals still spend significant amounts of time each day addressing the fundamentals. When you have a well-defined purpose, technical practice is rewarding and invigorating.

C Major Scale

A Melodic Minor Scale

C Major Arpeggio Exercise

A Minor Arpeggio Exercise

Chapter 7: Playing More Than One Note at a Time

So far (except for the chords on pages 34 and 40), we've been reading and playing only one note at a time. To prepare for more interesting repertoire, you need to begin reading and playing two or more notes at a time.

Let's start with the technical challenges of *playing* more than one note at a time before dealing with the task of *reading* multiple notes.

Multiple Fingers Working Together

First, we'll train the fingers to work together as a team, starting with a simple three-note chord on open strings (see Example 15). When playing chords, use free strokes, and keep all the basic principles of finger motion in mind.

The following steps will get you off to a good start.

1. Prepare the fingers on the strings in advance.

2. Pull through the strings, initiating the motion from the large knuckle joints.

3. After a good follow-through, empty tension from the fingers and allow them to return to their starting positions.

Thumb and Fingers Working Together

Next, let's get the fingers working with the thumb. We'll start with a four-note chord on open strings (see Example 16). Keep an eye out for the following as you try this.

1. Make sure your thumb passes outside your fingers; do not pinch together, or tuck your thumb into your palm—either of these techniques will slow you down.

2. With the motion originating from the knuckle joints, make sure your fingers and thumb follow through and then immediately release tension. Use the middle joints as necessary to achieve balance and fullness of sound.

3. And most importantly, when playing more than one note at a time, be sure the fingers are doing all the work and the hand is staying still. This is an area where your right hand may really want to "bounce" as it plucks—but don't let it. Be sure you're in control!

Hopefully, Example 16 is pretty easy for you, but don't underestimate the importance of your technique in all the examples presented here. Be sure to master each one, and don't be afraid to review with regularity, paying careful attention to your right hand.

Now that your hand knows how to move, we'll add some complicating factors, still using open strings only. In this next example, the thumb will move between the bass strings, and the *i* and *m* fingers will alternate on the 1st string. Note that the thumb must reach farther when the *i* finger is on the 1st string. Notice also that the stems on the treble notes are pointing upward and the stems on the bass notes are pointing downward. This means there are two distinct voices, or musical parts (see Practice Note 3 on page 38).

Below is an exercise with less time between the bass notes.

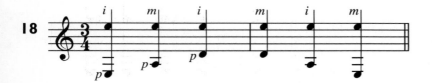

Now, let's try crossing the treble strings with the *i* and *m* fingers, keeping the thumb on the 6th string. You'll notice there are two right-hand fingering options. Crossing up with *m* is much more natural than with *i*, so you should work out fingerings that facilitate this. However, it is impossible to avoid occasionally crossing up with *i*, so you should also master that skill. Practice the exercise below with both fingerings.

And here is an open-string exercise with both the thumb and *i* and *m* fingers crossing strings.

Let's revisit the chromatic scale covered on page 29, this time with an E *drone*, or constant note, in the bass. Since your reading skills have improved, we'll also add open strings.

Hopefully, by now, you're feeling comfortable with the concept of playing more than one note at a time. The challenge for many people lies not so much in being able to play multiple notes, but in *reading* more than one note at a time. There is no quick solution to this—you just need to put in the time, and it will eventually get easier. With that in mind, following are a few pieces in which you'll have to identify notes that don't move in a predictable pattern. This will challenge you more than anything up to this point, so be sure to take your time with these pieces.

Greensleeves

This simple arrangement of a familiar tune features two notes at a time on downbeats only, allowing space for recovery and preparation as you build your skills in reading and playing simultaneous notes.

Practice Notes

1. This piece includes a pickup note (see page 36). Count beats 1 and 2 silently and then start playing on beat 3.

2. There are two voices in this piece. Take your time and practice slowly at first.

3. At the end of the piece appears the phrase *D.C. al Fine*. The abbreviation *D.C.* stands for *da capo*, which means to return to the beginning; *al Fine* means to play until the appearance of the word *Fine* (end).

Track 10 — Greensleeves

Traditional English Folk Song

Maestoso

The following piece by Mauro Giuliani (1781–1829) features the compositional technique of *counterpoint*, where two or more melodies are to be played simultaneously.

Practice Notes

1. If reading both voices at once is intimidating, read one voice at a time at first. This will help familiarize you with the pitches. However, it won't help your hand learn the moves it needs to make when both voices are working simultaneously. So, don't spend too much time doing this—just enough to get over the initial intimidation of reading two voices.

2. A general rule to follow for the right hand is to use *p* for the bass voice and the other fingers for the treble voice, but feel free to experiment with your own fingerings.

Track 11

Maestoso

Mauro Giuliani

♩ = 88

Etude in C

The following study by Sor is a great opportunity for you to start paying close attention to the duration of notes. Sometimes, it can be very tricky to stop a note from ringing, or to let one ring out for as long as it's supposed to.

Practice Notes

1. Notice all the eighth- and quarter-note rests that appear in one voice while the other voice is "speaking." Take the time to learn not only the right notes for this piece, but the right note durations as well. The result will be a clean-sounding little gem, as opposed to a messy diamond in the rough.

2. *Damping* is a technique used to stop notes from ringing. In this piece, we will need to use this technique extensively. For example, let's look at (and practice!) measures 2–3 (measure 1 is the first full measure, not the pickup). When you play the F on beat 2 of measure 2, be sure to stop the preceding A in the top voice from ringing. The simplest way to do that is to release the pressure from the left-hand finger that is fretting it, but leave it on the string to prevent it from vibrating. On the downbeat of measure 3, you'll need to do the same with the F in the bass voice of the preceding measure—just release the pressure from the left-hand finger, but leave it on the string.

3. Another way to damp a string is to place a right-hand finger or thumb on the string that is vibrating. For instance, when you play the F on the downbeat of measure 4, damp the open G string from the last beat of the preceding measure by momentarily touching your right-hand thumb to the string. Evaluate each situation to decide on the best approach for that passage. Remember, the simplest solution is usually the best.

4. Measure 7 features a tricky rhythm on the second half of beat 2—a dotted sixteenth note followed by a thirty-second note. An almost "skipping" quality is produced by the longer dotted sixteenth note followed by the shorter thirty-second note. Be sure to listen to the accompanying CD to hear how this rhythm is supposed to sound.

5. Notice the *D.C. al Fine* at the end. When you're playing from the beginning for the second time, do not take the repeats.

Etude in C

Track 12

Fernando Sor

Technical Supplements

The degree of difficulty rises quickly from here, so be sure to master the techniques discussed so far before moving on. If necessary, repeat exercises for several weeks and seek out other resources to expand your reading experience—whatever you have to do to acquire the skill to move forward in this book with confidence.

In the following arpeggios and scales, more technical aspects are introduced:

1. Practice all with both rest strokes and free strokes. Start with the stroke you feel more comfortable with, and then switch to the other.

2. Try the alternate right-hand fingerings suggested for the G Major scale on all of the scales from here on out. Though alternating between *i* and *a* is not extremely common in classical repertoire, the ability to do it will greatly improve your right-hand dexterity.

3. For the D Major scale, try adding the D bass notes on the downbeats as written—this will give you a bit more practice using the thumb and fingers together.

> **Note:** This book is not intended to be a comprehensive scale book, but the intention is to present some ideas for you to experiment with and apply to all your exercises as you wish. Be creative! It helps to keep your technical work interesting.

G Major Scale

D Major Scale

G Major Arpeggio Exercise

D Major Arpeggio Exercise

Chapter 8: Left-Hand Mobility

So far, we've covered how to use the right hand and how to use the left hand in 1st position. But music gets a lot more interesting when you're able to access the full range of notes on the guitar. So, let's talk about *shifting* with the left hand.

Shifting Up and Down the Neck

To "shift" is to move to a different *position*. A "position" generally refers to a four-fret area on the fingerboard, with the 1st finger assigned to the 1st fret of the position, the 2nd finger to the 2nd fret, etc. For instance, 5th position refers to frets 5–8, with the 1st finger assigned to the 5th fret, the 2nd finger to the 6th fret, etc. Note that these fingering assignments are just general guidelines and by no means apply to every situation.

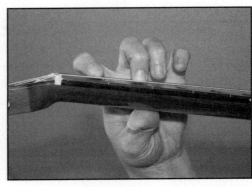

Fig. 1: Correct thumb placement for 1st position.

The thumb is a principal component of successful shifting. As discussed in Chapter 5, your thumb should be positioned behind the neck, midway between the 1st and 6th strings and approximately one fret higher than the first fret of the position you're in. In 1st position, that means your thumb will be approximately behind the 2nd fret (see Fig. 1 to the right). In 5th position, your thumb will be behind the 6th fret (see Fig. 2 to the right). This allows you to balance all your fingers and achieve the greatest reach with minimal effort.

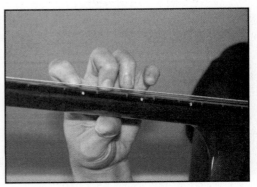

Fig. 2: Correct thumb placement for 5th position.

As you shift up the neck, do *not* move the fingers first and then drag the rest of your hand and arm behind. This results in a different orientation between the hand and the neck, and will result in inaccurate playing (see Fig. 3 to the right). Your goal as you move up and down the neck (once your great initial position is defined) is to use your shoulder as a fulcrum and maintain the relationship between the guitar neck and your elbow, wrist, hand, and fingers.

Fig. 3: The result of improper shifting to 5th position.

Other factors that are critical in shifting are:

- The release of the last note (or notes) before the shift

- The energy used during the shift

- The quality of the landing on the new note (or notes)

The release of the last note before the shift must be timed carefully with the movement of the arm to avoid buzzes, notes that are cut too short, or unintentional sliding notes as you move.

The shift itself must have an appropriate amount of energy (speed), which varies greatly depending on the context of the piece. In general, aim to make slow, careful movements—do not rush, especially when learning a new move.

Finally, do not "grab" at the new note (or notes) in the new position—this will inevitably produce an accent, along with excess tension (which comes with a slew of other problems). Be aware of exactly what fret you're shifting to, and be sure to arrive exactly at the intended spot: no overshifting (often a sign of excess tension) or undershifting (which can be a result of hesitation or confusion).

Let's try a variation on a chromatic scale, which shifts up one fret every other note. (Note that when you come to the end of each of the examples in this section, you should also practice shifting backwards.) This is a great introduction to small shifts. As you are shifting, don't worry too much about making it sound legato—be more attentive to the motion and relative position of your left hand. Notice in the example that the positions are marked with Roman numerals: I = 1st position, II = 2nd position, etc. (See Roman Numeral Review below.)

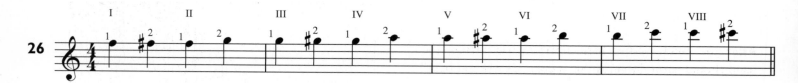

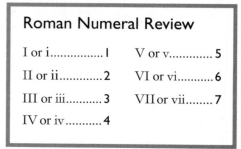

Roman Numeral Review

I or i	1	V or v	5
II or ii	2	VI or vi	6
III or iii	3	VII or vii	7
IV or iv	4		

When shifting one fret feels easy, and your left hand is able to maintain good position throughout the shifts, try the following variations on the exercise: shifting two frets at a time, and then three frets at a time.

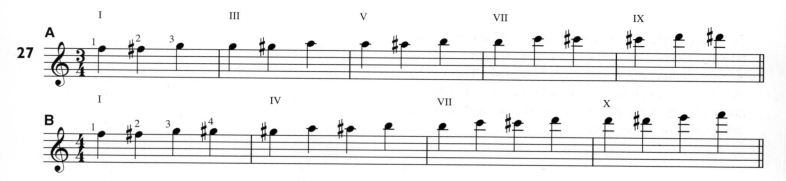

As shifting becomes a bigger part of your playing, it can be very helpful to write all of the position shifts into your music. This heightens your awareness of exactly where and when to shift, which increases the likelihood that your thumb will end up in the right spot. When you shift without thinking (more common than you'd expect), the thumb tends to lag behind, messing up your left-hand technique.

In this chapter, all positions will be indicated. For the rest of the book, however, you'll need to write them in on your own—only the less obvious ones will be marked. In general, you can figure out which position you're supposed to be in through other clues in the fingering. You won't need to mark all positions forever, but maintaining awareness of where you are going is very important while you're still developing your technique.

Shifting Within a Position

So far, we've talked about shifting up and down the neck. But there are also shifts of the hand within any position. This type of shift is required particularly when any two fingers play on the same fret. We spoke earlier about keeping the inside of the left palm parallel with the neck of the guitar. This is a good general rule, but when two fingers are playing notes on the same fret (different strings), your hand will rotate a bit toward the nut. This should, however, feel like an alternative position, not home base.

When two fingers are playing notes on the same fret, the hand will rotate a bit toward the nut.

After the need for this hand position has passed, the hand should naturally return to the parallel "home-base" position.

"Home-base" position.

For many guitarists, this takes a lot of attention and training, as they have developed a home-base position already oriented towards the nut. This works fine in many popular styles, but it will not serve you well in classical guitar playing. Keep an eye on this as you work through the repertoire in this book.

Carulli Arpeggio Studies

The following preludes by Ferdinando Carulli (1770–1841) incorporate subtle shifts within position, as well as small shifts to other positions. Be sure that you're using good left-hand technique on the familiar left-hand chord shapes (not reverting to any old habits) and that you're using great contact points and follow-through with your right hand.

The Barre

The first two preludes include *barres*. A barre is the fretting of multiple strings at the same fret with one finger, and it is accomplished by laying that finger flat across the strings to be fretted. Most guitarists of any style have some experience with barres, but it's worth re-evaluating how you use your hand when playing them. Here are a couple of pointers:

1. Avoid excess tension, especially in the thumb behind the neck.

2. Be aware that barres need not (and should not) always lay precisely flat on the fingerboard. Your finger may roll slightly in one direction or another depending on what other notes are being played with the remaining fingers.

3. Many barres are made easier by 1) rolling a little to the left side of the 1st finger (99 out of 100 barres are done with the 1st finger), and 2) moving the left elbow in a little closer to your side. The combination of these two adjustments provides more leverage, thus requiring less finger/hand strength, or tension. Of course, after playing a barre chord, always make sure you return your left hand and arm to the correct home base.

The barres in these pieces are relatively simple, but as we progress, they will become more involved. Take this opportunity to see if there's anything you can do to help your hand operate more efficiently while barring.

Note: Barres are indicated with a "B" followed by the fret and number of strings to be barred. For example, BV_3 means that three strings should be barred at the 5th fret.

Guide Fingers

A *guide finger* is a finger that plays notes on the same string when moving from one note or chord to the next. Guide fingers help to ensure smooth shifts and transitions, and may be indicated in written music by a small dash preceding the finger number. For instance, in measure 4 of "Prelude in A," you will see the fingering indication -1 preceding the second sixteenth note. This tells us we are moving our 1st finger up or down on the same string to arrive at this note (in this case, we are moving the 1st finger up from the G♯ in measure 3).

Prelude in A

Ferdinando Carulli

Prelude in A Minor

Track 14

Ferdinando Carulli

* This is a *sextuplet*, which consists of six notes in the time of four. In other words, these six sixteenth notes are spread evenly across the time of one beat.

Prelude in G

Ferdinando Carulli

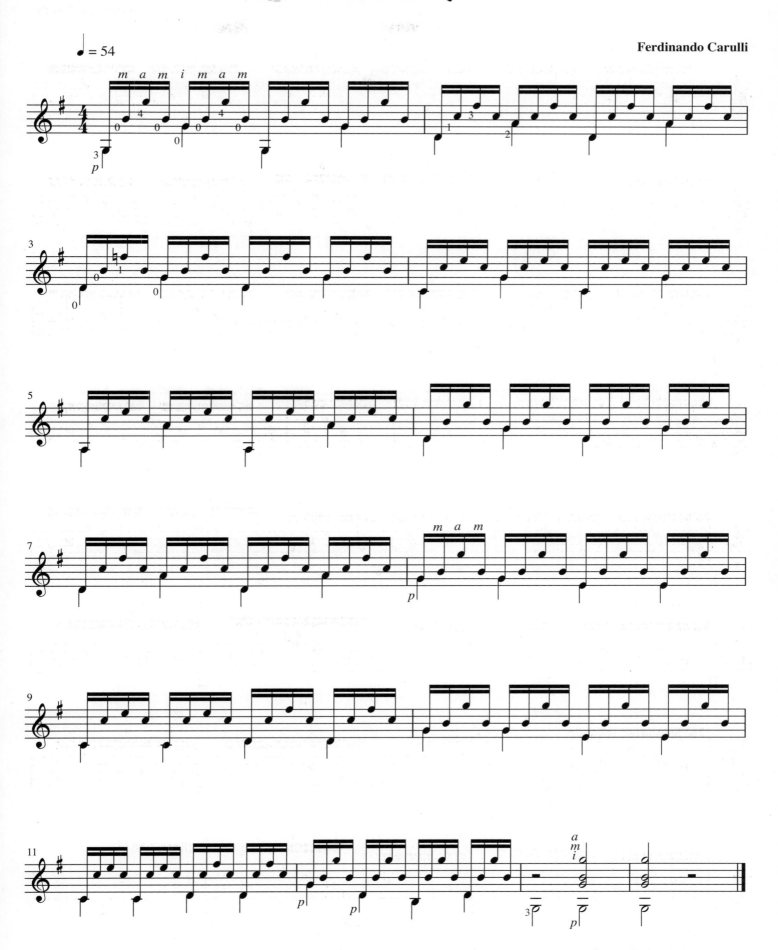

Prelude in E

Ferdinando Carulli

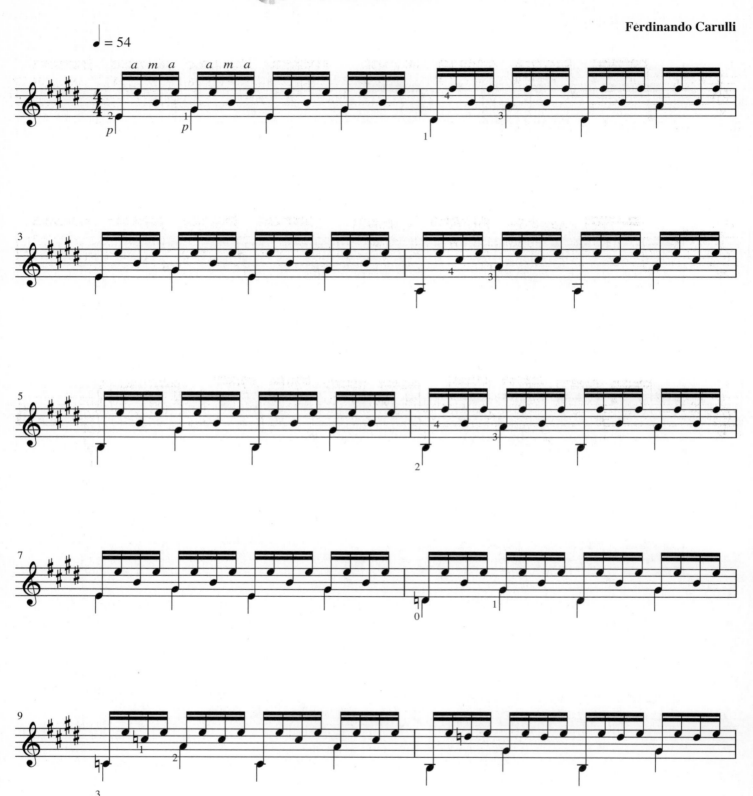

Chapter 9: Putting It All Together

In Chapter 7, you learned about playing more than one note at a time; in Chapter 8, you learned about shifting. Let's try some examples that incorporate all your new skills. Learn these pieces slowly. First, study them to be sure you understand all the elements. Approach them (and any pieces you learn) one phrase at a time. Quality repetition will help the movements to "stick" better in your brain and in your fingers. If you do full run-throughs, by the time you get to the end, you'll forget what you discovered that made earlier measures easier to play. Repeat things in small phrases, and you'll reach your end goal much more quickly. If you find that you have the common problem of being much more comfortable with the beginning of the piece than the end, you might try learning the piece starting with the last phrase first, and then working your way backward through the piece. Be creative in solving your learning challenges.

Sicilienne

Practice Notes

1. This piece by Carulli is primarily in 1st position, with just one shift occurring twice. However, within the 1st position, there are plenty of changes to the orientation of the left hand. Always make sure you're returning to the correct home base after you've moved your hand to reach a chord.

2. Also, in measures 4 and 20, notice the small note preceding beat 2. This is a *grace note*, which we'll be covering on page 80. For now, feel free to just leave that note out, or, if you are already familiar with grace notes, go ahead and include it.

3. The time signature for this piece is $\frac{6}{8}$, which means there are six beats per measure with the eighth note getting one beat. $\frac{6}{8}$ time can be counted: 1–2–3–4–5–6 or 1–2–3–**2**–2–3. In the first case, the pulse is on the 1 and 4, and in the second, it is on the 1 and 2. $\frac{6}{8}$ is an example of a *compound meter*, where each beat, or pulse, is divisible by three. Other examples of compound meter are $\frac{9}{8}$ and $\frac{12}{8}$.

4. Notice there are a number of symbols and markings we have not seen until now. Most of these relate to the dynamics of the piece, and you will learn about these in greater detail starting on page 103.

p	= *piano*	= soft	
pp	= *pianissimo*	= very soft	
f	= *forte*	= loud	
	= *crescendo*	= gradually get louder	
	= *decrescendo*	= gradually get softer	

5. The symbol ⌢ is a *fermata*, which tells you to pause or hold a note longer than its normal value.

Sicilienne

Ferdinando Carulli

Larghetto Espressivo

This lyrical piece stays mostly in 1st position, with a few reaches to the 5th fret and, for the final note, the 7th fret.

Practice Notes

1. Be aware that the shifts of position up and down the neck may not be as much of a challenge as keeping the voices connected while you shift between chords within a position.

2. Think musically—not just technically—as you move from chord to chord, and keep the melody flowing.

3. Arcing above measures 1–4 and 16–20 are curved lines called *phrase markings*. These indicate that the marked passages are to be considered complete musical thoughts and should be played legato, or as smoothly and connected as possible.

Track 18 *Larghetto Espressivo*

Ferdinando Carulli

Moderato

Following is a more playful piece by Carulli.

Practice Notes

1. You will find only a few small shifts of position but many opportunities for creative use of dynamics. Though we haven't yet discussed dynamics in detail, use your imagination as you come up with the musical plan for this piece. Then, you can revisit this composition (and others like it) after you've explored dynamics and colors later in the book (Chapter 13). Note that there is a dynamic marking in this piece that we haven't yet seen:

   mf = *mezzo forte* = moderately loud

2. "Moderato" contains a few musical indications that we haven't seen yet. For instance, beat 2 of the second measure has an *accent* mark (>) on both voices. This instructs you to emphasize these notes, or play them louder than the surrounding notes. And when you see a dot above or below a note, as in measure 12, it indicates that the notes are to be played *staccato* (short, detached; see page 106 for more details).

3. You will also see some musical indications in Italian. These phrases help communicate the composer's intentions for interpreting the piece, and they should be given careful consideration.

   - *poco rit.* = slow down a little. (*Poco* means "little"; *rit.* is short for *ritardando* and means "slow down.")

   - *a tempo* = return to the original tempo, or speed.

   - *e sempre legato* = continuously legato, or connected. (*Sempre* means "always.")

Track 19 ♪ Moderato

Ferdinando Carulli

Vals

Next is a piece by guitarist/composer José Ferrer (1835–1916).

Practice Notes

1. This piece is a *waltz*. A waltz is a dance usually in $\frac{3}{4}$ time, but it can appear (as it does here) in $\frac{3}{8}$ as well. In $\frac{3}{8}$ time, there are three beats per measure with the eighth note getting one beat. $\frac{3}{8}$ can be counted 1, 2, 3; 1, 2, 3, etc. However, because this is a compound meter (where each beat is divisible by three), the pulse occurs on the first beat of each measure; so it is like one big beat per measure.

2. "Vals" moves in and out of relatively common chord shapes that, depending on your experience, you may be familiar with.

3. Guide fingers (see page 52) are utilized in this piece to ensure smooth position shifts. For example, in measures 5–7, the left-hand pinky (the 4th finger) remains on the high-E string but moves from the 7th fret to the 5th fret to the 3rd fret.

Track 20 *Vals*

José Ferrer

Prelude

This prelude by Franceso Molino (1775–1847) features several barres.

Practice Notes

1. As discussed previously, by slightly pulling the elbow in toward the body, you gain some leverage for the 1st finger that is holding down the barre. Use the weight of your left arm to help you barre efficiently, instead of just "squeezing."

2. In measure 4, notice the sharp sign in parentheses on the second half of beat 4. This is a *courtesy accidental*, which is a reminder about the correct pitch of a note. Remember, accidentals apply only to the particular octave in which they are notated. In this case, even though the C was sharped on beat 1, it is in a different voice; so, to avoid confusion, the courtesy accidental was used to remind us that the C is still sharped.

Track 21 *Prelude*

Francesco Molino

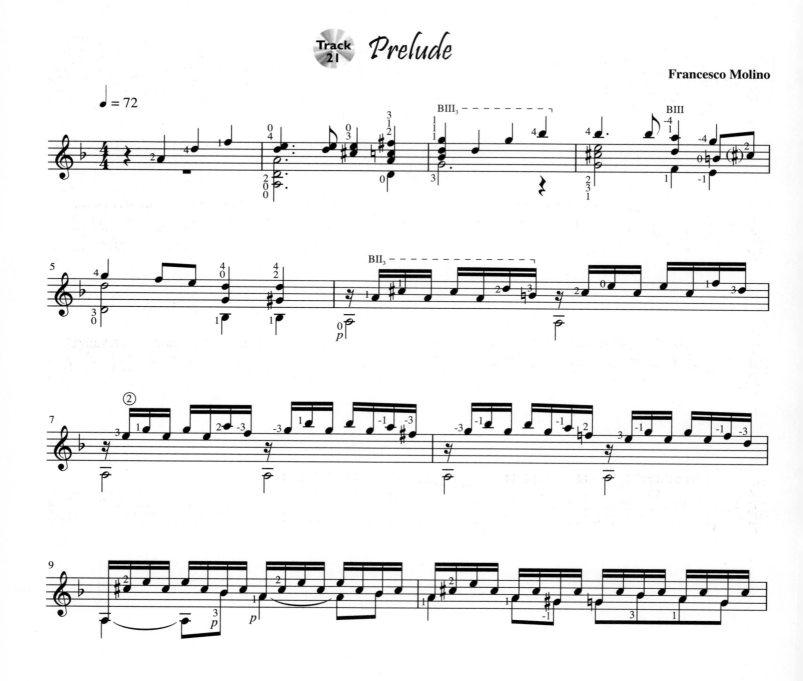

Andante Agitato

This is the most challenging Carulli composition presented so far, and it is another good example of a piece to revisit after you've worked through the chapter dealing with dynamics (Chapter 13).

Practice Notes

1. Take your time on this one and really practice all the fingerings. Don't guess which finger is supposed to go where—work it all out beforehand.

2. Observe all the dynamic markings in this piece. There is one you have not yet learned:

   $\boldsymbol{f\!f}$ = *fortissimo* = very loud

3. Pay special attention to the articulation markings as well. Remember, when a curved line arcs above or below a group of notes, it means those notes are part of a phrase and should be played legato. Another way to indicate a legato feel, where the notes are held for their full value or even beyond, is *tenuto*. Tenuto is shown as a straight line above or below a note, as in the first beat of measure 5. (See page 106 for more on this.)

Track 22 **Andante Agitato**

Ferdinando Carulli

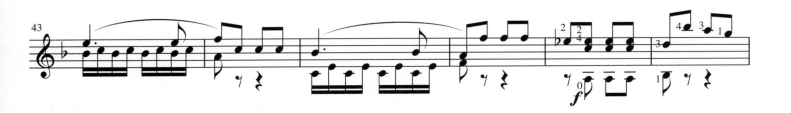

Romanza

This is another one of the most popular pieces for classical guitar. It is also a great study for arpeggios, barre chords, and shifting. There are a couple of shifts worth discussing below.

Practice Notes

1. Measure 19 contains an unusual fingering on beat 3—this is intended as preparation for the upcoming shift. If you play beat 3 of measure 19 with your 1st finger (as would be natural), you will never be able to connect that G♯ to the downbeat of the next measure. By fretting the G♯ with the 2nd finger, your 1st finger is free to prepare for the upcoming barre. This will still be a difficult shift, but this fingering gives you a better chance for success.

2. If, after much practice, you still find the passage mentioned above to be too difficult, you may choose to simplify it by changing the bass note in measure 20. If you play an open A instead of the F♯ on the 6th string, you won't need a barre at all, and this part becomes much easier. The original harmony is richer, but it's always good to have options.

3. The shift into measure 22 is difficult as well. Study it very slowly and carefully, and always allow yourself a little extra time to make the shift—better to give yourself this time and accomplish the shift with a pleasing tone than to land there precisely on time but with a sloppy or unpleasant result. It can be helpful to practice the left-hand fingerings without the shift (i.e. with the wrong notes) as an exercise, so you can work on mastering the fingerings and mastering the shift separately. Then, add in the shift to the correct notes.

4. Note the symbol 𝄪 in measure 21. This is a *double sharp*, which tells you to raise the pitch of a note by two half steps. A C𝄪 is fingered the same as a D.

Track 23 *Romanza*

Anonymous

𝅘𝅥. = 84

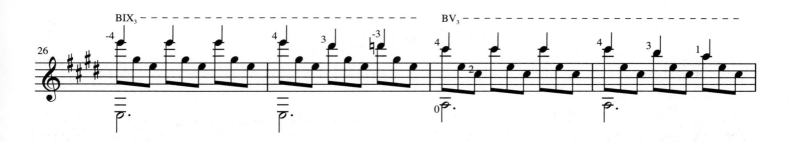

Technical Supplements

This version of the A Major scale includes a three-fret shift, which occurs while your right hand is playing the open B in measure 3. This makes it possible to connect the line smoothly and without much extra effort. Make sure your palm remains parallel to the neck as you shift.

A Major Scale

The following version of the E Major scale is written in a *moveable* scale form. If you have experience in other styles of guitar, you likely know many moveable scale forms (like the box shapes for the minor pentatonic scale). When a scale is moveable, it means no open strings are used, so the pattern can be moved to any part of the fingerboard and remain intact. For instance, if we moved the fingering pattern for this E Major scale up one fret, we would have an F Major scale.

Many moveable forms involve some sort of small shift, as is the case below, which has a one-fret *compression shift* (sometimes called a *squeeze shift*) where your hand compresses to allow the 1st finger to arrive one fret higher, as opposed to reaching . But be sure when performing this kind of shift that the entire hand moves—even if you can actually play the notes without moving the whole hand. This is about creating good habits. The better your habits, the more accurate you'll be.

E Major Scale (Moveable Form)

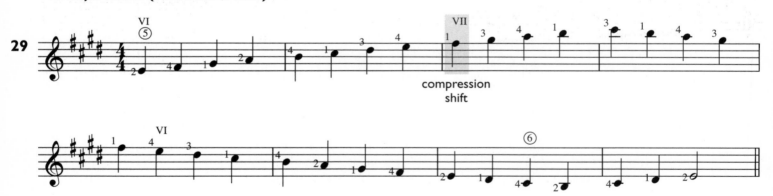

The following arpeggios involve more complex right-hand patterns, as well as big shifts, which are not so easy to connect. Play slowly, and don't be obsessed with creating legato at first. Rather, be sure your movement is good. Then go back and correct any problems with your legato.

A Major Arpeggio

E Major Arpeggio

Chapter 10: Slurs

Most string instruments use the *slurring* technique, though it sounds different on a guitar than on a bowed string instrument. A slur on the guitar (which is the same in all styles) is indicated by a curved line ⌒ between two different notes on the same string. The first note is articulated by the right hand, but the second note is sounded by an action of the left hand only. There are two kinds of slurs: *ascending* and *descending*.

Ascending Slurs

Ascending slurs (also called *hammer-ons*) involve plucking the first of the two notes with the right hand, and then tapping, or "hammering on" to the second (higher-pitched) note with a left-hand finger.

In all slurs, it is critical for the primary motion to be made by the finger, not the entire hand. With ascending slurs, it is also important for the lower finger to remain in place when the higher finger articulates the second note. Trying to coordinate the lifting of that lower finger while placing the higher is a nearly impossible task, and completely unnecessary. Save yourself the trouble and learn this technique right the first time.

If you are struggling to hear the second note, you may have one of two problems:

1. Inaccuracy—If you don't hit the string with the sweet spot of your fingertip (exactly where you'd normally play), you won't produce enough sound, no matter how hard the motion. Where your finger lands on the string is extremely important and must be performed with accuracy.

2. If your placement is good, but you're still not getting enough sound, then likely you are "placing" your finger, as opposed to "striking," or "tapping," the string with sufficient force from the knuckle joint. A hammer-on is a percussive move—don't be afraid to hit it!

Descending Slurs

Descending slurs (also called *pull-offs*) are executed by plucking the first note with the right hand, and then, with sufficient force from the middle joint of the finger that is fretting that first note, pulling inward toward the palm to articulate a lower-pitched note on the same string. Unless pulling off to an open string, it is critical for *both* fingers to be in place before beginning the slur.

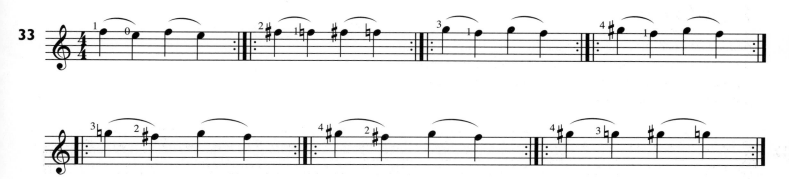

With descending slurs, you need to watch for the dynamic balance between the two notes. Some players don't "pull" enough to set the lower note vibrating, resulting in insufficient sound. Others pull too hard and get a snapping sound, which is undesirable. Listen carefully to see if you are prone to one or the other tendency, and work to improve the balance of your descending slurs.

Two Short Pieces

The following short pieces by Dionisio Aguado (1784–1849) and Joseph Küffner (1776–1856) are great for working on slurs.

Practice Notes

1. When executing the slurs in these pieces, be sure that your left hand stays as still as possible—let the fingers do all the work.

2. Strive to maintain the dynamic balance between the notes in each slur.

Track 24 *Allegro*

Dionisio Aguado

Rondo

Joseph Küffner

Divertimento

Once you're comfortable with slurs in a single position, you can start to practice them in the context of shifting passages, like those found in this piece by Antonio Cano (1811–1897).

Practice Notes

1. Executing slurs in shifting passages presents an extra challenge for your left hand. While working on this piece, be sure to maintain good hand position, with the inside of your palm parallel to the neck of the guitar as you move between positions.

Track 26 *Divertimento*

Antonio Cano

Chapter 11: Ornaments

An *ornament* in music is much like an ornament in life—it is a decorative accent. In the musical sense, an ornament normally embellishes a melody. We can create different types of ornaments using a combination of slur techniques.

Grace Notes

Grace notes are the simplest of the ornaments, involving a quick ascending or descending slur just prior to a principal note. The grace note is notated smaller than the note it precedes, and it often has a line going through the stem (see right). With no countable note value of its own, the grace note can be executed *before* the beat (with the principal note then falling on the beat), or *on* the beat (with the principal note then falling just after the beat). Grace notes are typically written before the beat, but the notation often does not reflect a clarity of intention on the part of the composer. Use your musical intuition to judge what is best in each particular scenario—this general advice will apply for all types of ornaments.

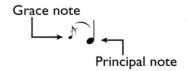

Trill

Perhaps the most common ornament is the *trill* (*tr* or ~). Using a series of rapid hammer-ons and pull-offs, a trill alternates between two notes: a principal note and its *upper neighbor tone*, which is either a whole step or half step above, depending on the key signature. The number of times you go back and forth is up to you, but, typically, playing each note twice (in alternation) is a good starting point.

Depending on the style of the piece, sometimes it is desirable to start a trill on the higher of the two pitches (the ornamental note), and sometimes it is desirable to start on the lower of the two pitches (the principal note). Most trills can begin on the upper note, but, often, even experts can't agree on what is stylistically correct in certain situations. Trust yourself—your ear will generally tell you on which note to begin the trill and how long it should be held. You can also listen to musicians you respect and experiment with their interpretations of the trill.

To execute a trill, pluck the first note with your right hand, then use ascending and descending slurs to articulate the remaining notes.

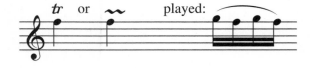

Mordent

A *mordent* ~ is an ornament similar to a trill, but simpler. Begin by plucking the principal note with the right hand, then hammer on to the upper neighbor tone and immediately return to the principal note using a pull-off.

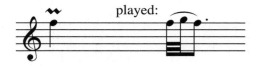

Note: Don't let ornaments interrupt the rhythm of a piece. It's easy to get caught up in the moment and accidentally turn a measure of $\frac{3}{4}$ time into common time. Watch out for this unintended consequence with all ornaments, but especially trills. Also, remember that the quality of sound must remain pleasing. If your ornament is not working well in the piece, practice it independently, but leave it out when you do run-throughs or performances. Ornaments are supposed to make the piece more attractive, not draw attention to flaws!

Valtz

This short piece by Aguado is a great introduction to ornamentation with the grace note.

Practice Notes

1. Play each grace note on the beat (at the same time you are plucking the chord in the upper voice), with the principal bass note following immediately after. To execute these grace notes before the beat would be not only extremely difficult, but would sound awkward as well.

Track 27 *Valtz*

Dionisio Aguado

Ländler

Following is a composition by Johann Kasper Mertz (1806–1856).

Practice Notes

1. Notice the mordents in measures 17 and 21. Here, they are fully notated using grace notes.

2. Because this piece is an arpeggio study, it may be a challenge to make the melody stand out from the "accompaniment." Be sure to practice bringing out the melodic line, indicated with accent marks. In addition, the marking sf is an abbreviation for *sforzando*, or a sudden, strong accent.

3. "Ländler" primarily stays in the 1st and 2nd positions, with just a couple of migrations up to 7th position for the D Major chord. Look before you leap!

Track 28 *Ländler*

Johann Kaspar Mertz

Andante

This short piece by Aguado is excellent practice for extended grace notes, as well as the *glissando* technique, which consists of sliding from one note to another.

Glissando

A glissando (or "gliss") is indicated by a straight line between two notes (see right) and is executed by sliding a guide finger from one note to another note on the same string.

When performing a gliss, the guide finger maintains pressure on the fingerboard to produce a smooth, continuous sound between the two notes. But when shifting positions *without* the gliss technique, the finger releases its pressure from the fingerboard while maintaining contact with the string. In the latter case, you will hear two separate notes with no sliding sound in between.

A gliss should be quick and light, so that you aren't focused too heavily on each chromatic note in between the principal notes of the slide—it's a graceful way to travel between two notes, nothing more important than that. Avoid too much tension in the left hand, which not only makes for an awkward shift, but also a heavy glissando.

To avoid overshifting, always be aware of the glissando's target arrival fret. If you're frequently missing your destination, slow down and make sure your eyes are on the target fret before you arrive.

Practice Notes

1. As with all ornaments, the grace notes should add to the beauty of the piece. Keep them graceful and light.

2. Note the glissando in measure 4, where the F♯ on the 4th string slides to the B on the same string. This slide helps connect the two chords and makes for a smooth transition. (Note: On the recording, the glissando is not used, but this is a matter of interpretation. Experiment with this passage on your own using this technique.)

3. In measures 6 and 7, be careful to hold all notes for their full durations. The melody notes on top must be held while the chords change underneath. This takes practice to master, so be patient.

4. The term *marcato* (see measures 13–14) instructs you to stress or emphasize the marked notes.

5. Be attentive to the rhythm of this piece, which requires a strong sense of pulse throughout.

Track 29

Andante

Dionisio Aguado

Allegretto

This piece by Ferrer features a lot of shifting and many slurs.

Practice Notes

1. The slurs in this piece are primarily ascending, with the exception of measure 28, which includes two descending slurs in a row (pluck once, pull off twice).

2. Don't forget to mark in all your position shifts, and be conscious of maintaining great left-hand technique.

3. Note the harmonic (harm.) in measure 31. To learn more about this technique, see page 93.

Track 30 *Allegretto*

José Ferrer

Etude

This etude by Cano spans much of the fingerboard, develops arpeggio technique, and includes many descending slurs.

Practice Notes

1. Watch for recurring arpeggio patterns, like the D Major arpeggio in measures 1, 4, 5, 12, and 13.

2. Be particularly mindful of the quality of sound when pulling off to an open string, as in beat 4 of measure 7. Pulling off to an open string can cause that note to "pop out" in unpleasant ways, so be very careful not to pull off too aggressively in those situations.

Track 31

Etude

Albert Cano

♩ = 52

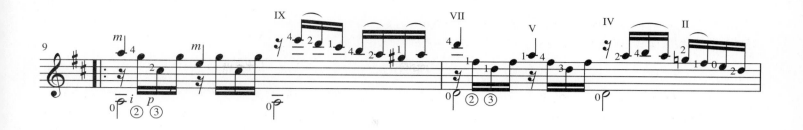

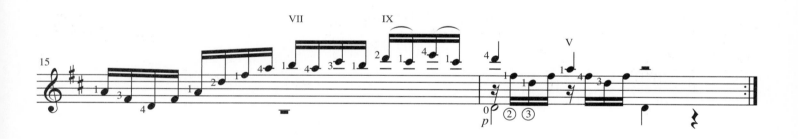

Aria

This composition by Giuseppe Antonio Brescianello (1690–1758) is a great opportunity to experiment with ornaments.

Practice Notes

1. Measures 4 and 20 include a grace note each. Play these ornaments on the beat, along with the accompanying bass notes, with the principal notes occurring quickly and lightly afterward.

2. Watch for the trill in measure 11, where you rapidly alternate (using pull-offs and hammer-ons) between the 1st fret (with the 1st finger) and the open 1st string. This is accomplished while the 3rd finger holds the G bass note underneath.

3. As you become more advanced with the trilling technique, experiment with adding trills of your own—especially the second time through each section.

Track 32 · **Aria**

Giuseppe Antonio Brescianello

Technical Supplements

Chromatic Scale with Slurs

A Major Arpeggio with Slurs

Chapter 12: Special "Tricks" and Techniques

The classical guitar has a number of cool "tricks" for the enjoyment of players and audiences alike. Let's look at some of these now.

Pizzicato

For players of bowed string instruments, *pizzicato* (or *pizz.*) is the technique of plucking a note with a right-hand finger rather than using the bow. This results in a short, sharp sound, rather than the sustained tone of a bowed note. Since guitar is not played with a bow, the pizzicato technique is a bit different. Pizzicato on the classical guitar means to play with a muted sound. To accomplish this, we place the outside of the right-hand palm just forward of the bridge—enough to deaden the sound just slightly—and then play as normal with the right-hand fingers.

Correct right-hand placement for pizzicato.

This technique mutes the string and creates a different quality of sound. Generally, you want to be sure that you can still hear the pitch as you do this and that it doesn't become too dead (where all you hear is the percussive "plunk" of the string). To accomplish this, be sure you aren't too far forward on the string.

Likewise, if you're hearing too much natural note and not enough pizzicato, you're likely drifting behind the bridge, where you'll lose the muting effect. Getting the hand in just the right spot is a technical challenge, so extra practice is suggested: Try any of the simpler scales presented earlier in this book (or even just open strings), applying the pizzicato technique with both your thumb and fingers.

Bartók Pizzicato

Bartók pizzicato is a unique and effective technique in which you pull the string out with the right hand and release it, allowing it to smack against the fingerboard to create a loud, percussive sound. You can do this on any open string or fretted note.

You won't find this technique in older pieces, but it is fun to experiment with and is becoming more common in modern-day repertoire. (Plus, it always gets a great audience response!)

Bartók pizzicato is notated like this:

Golpe

Used in both classical and flamenco technique, *golpe* involves the percussive tapping on the guitar to create a drum-like effect.

The golpe technique (often indicated with a ✕ above the staff) is accomplished by tapping a rhythm on the bridge or a variety of places on the top, sides, or back of the guitar. By tapping on the fingerboard, a distinctive "clicking" sound is generated from the vibrating strings.

Feel free to experiment with different approaches. You can try:

- tapping with your open hand (mostly fingers) on the top, back, and sides of the guitar

- knocking with your knuckles on the back and sides of the guitar

- tapping with your fingernails on the sides of the guitar

There are no rules, other than be careful not to damage your guitar! Experiment and enjoy the process of discovery—you never know what it may inspire in you.

Harmonics

Harmonics are clear, bell-like tones that can be produced on the guitar using a combination of left- and right-hand techniques. There are two kinds of harmonics: *natural* and *artificial*.

Natural Harmonics

Natural harmonics are the easier of the two types and are produced by lightly touching any of the strings directly over the fretwire at the 5th, 7th, 9th, and 12th frets. You can also create natural harmonics at lots of other frets, though, in some these locations, it is more difficult to produce clean and ringing tones.

Let's start by playing a natural harmonic at the 12th fret, which is the midway point between the nut and bridge.

1. Place any left-hand finger directly over the 12th fret—not behind the fret, where you'd typically place the finger to fret a note—and rest it on the string lightly, without pressing down.

2. Then, with the right hand, pluck as you normally would, and immediately lift the left-hand finger off the string. If you don't lift the finger soon enough, you'll get a dead note; if you lift it too soon, you'll just sound the open string.

Work on your timing until you create the perfect harmonic. You can experiment with harmonics using different left-hand fingers, on different strings, and at different frets. This technique is easy once you get the hang of it—just be sure to work on finding the exact location on the fingerboard that will give you the best results. The 12th fret produces the most pure tone, and as you work back towards the 5th fret, you'll notice that, sometimes, the cleanest harmonics are produced slightly in front of or slightly behind the fret. If you're not getting the same clarity in your harmonics at the 5th fret as you do at the 12th, experiment with exactly where to place your finger to yield the cleanest result possible.

Artificial Harmonics

Natural harmonics limit you to only certain pitches that can be produced at certain frets. However, we can create harmonics at any fret by using artificial harmonics. Here's how to do it:

1. With a left-hand finger, fret the note you'd like to play as a harmonic—fret it down one octave from how you want it to sound. For example, let's use D on the 2nd string, 3rd fret. Fret it as you would a normal note, placing your left-hand finger behind the fret and pressing down.

2. Now, locate the fret that is 12 frets higher than the 3rd fret (12+3=15) and place the tip of your right-hand index finger (*i*) directly over the top of the fret (as you would to produce a natural harmonic with your left hand). By doing this, you are creating the midway point between the fretted note and the bridge—in other words, you are "artificially" creating a harmonic point.

3. With your left hand planted on the fretted note at the 3rd fret, and the *i* finger resting gently on the string at the 15th fret, pluck the string with you're *a* finger, immediately lifting your *i* finger off the string (as you did with the left hand for natural harmonics). Be sure that your left-hand finger remains in place on the 3rd fret to maintain the pitch.

This technique definitely takes some practice! Begin by working on individual notes without concern for time or rhythm. If you can cross strings and play the Technical Supplements (Examples 38A–C) on page 102, you are ready to try a piece that incorporates artificial harmonics. Remember, whenever you encounter a piece with artificial harmonics, a good approach is to learn it first with regular notes only, so the left hand is clear about its job before introducing the challenge of the right hand.

Notation for Harmonics

In classical repertoire, the notation for harmonics is inconsistent. Often, a diamond-shaped notehead indicates a harmonic. Some composers use regular-shaped noteheads with the indication "harm." placed above the note. Some composers show the natural note that would sound if fretting that fret; others show the actual pitch of the harmonic. You'll learn to decipher the harmonic "code" by following the fingerings, which are often your best indication of what the composer intends. Reading harmonics can be intimidating at first, but once you understand what's being asked of you and you have a basic command of the technique, they shouldn't be a problem for you.

In this book, you will see the natural note that would sound and the indication "harm." placed over the notes. You will also see the designation *8va*, which tells you that the actual pitch is one octave higher than the written note. For example:

Pepe Romero (b. 1944) is a virtuoso classical and flamenco guitarist known for his dazzling technique and fiery musical interpretations. Making his debut at the age of 7, his only guitar teacher was his father, the famous guitarist Celedonio Romero. The Romero Guitar Quartet, originally comprised of Celedonio, Pepe, and Pepe's brothers Celin and Angel, is one of the most popular guitar ensembles of all time and is also known as "The Royal Family of the Guitar."

Manuel Barrueco (b. 1952) is a Cuban-born classical guitarist, who, having moved to the United States as a teenager, made his debut at Carnegie Hall in 1974. Known for his versatility, expressive interpretations, and wide-ranging repertoire, he has also collaborated with artists and composers as diverse as Arvo Pärt, Steven Stucky, Al Di Meola, Steve Morse, and Andy Summers (The Police).

La Chasse

This piece by Coste is great for practicing harmonics.

Practice Notes

1. Harmonics are included in measures 10–12 and
   35–37. These are all natural harmonics played at the
   12th and 7th frets. Practice these passages slowly
   to ensure clean, ringing tones.

La Chasse

Napoléon Coste

Tremolo

Developing a good *tremolo* (repeated notes in rapid succession) technique requires patience and lots of hard work. Tremolo is executed by playing the right-hand pattern *p-a-m-i*, usually with *p* on a bass note and *a-m-i* on a repeated note in the upper voice.

In the "big picture," the thumb plays a bass line and the fingers carry a "sustained" melody.

You'll encounter the following challenges as you study tremolo:

1. **The thumb is our strongest digit and wants to dominate the piece, when, generally, the melody is in the fingers.** So, you need to work in order to create a healthy balance between the thumb and fingers.

2. **Rhythm.** Most people tend to develop certain combinations of fingers that move a little too quickly, or a little too sluggishly. It is critical that the distances between all four notes of the pattern be equal. Beware of the galloping tremolo!

3. **Tone.** When playing fast, a lot of players tend to throw good technique out the window. Using your refined contact points (that we worked on earlier in this book) will ensure that you maintain a high standard for tone when learning to play tremolo. Letting the fingers fly without thought likely ensures the opposite.

4. **Dynamic balance between the fingers.** We already talked about how the thumb can dominate over the fingers and how you want to avoid this. You also need to avoid any finger dominating over the others—the idea here is equality of the fingers, which is what creates the sustained sound. Most people have one finger that tends to play louder than the others (often *m*). Listen as you play to ensure all the fingers are working together to create a sustained sound that is dynamically even.

In learning tremolo, it is recommended that you start very slowly. Make sure your technique remains strong and that you're considering all the points on the checklist above. It is more difficult to play tremolo on an inner string (specifically, the 2nd and 3rd) than on the 1st string, so be sure to practice this technique on the inner strings.

Try the following exercise, which features tremolo on the 2nd string and a wandering bass line.

Scott Tennant is a world-renowned concert artist and teacher, and is a founding member of the Grammy®-winning Los Angeles Guitar Quartet (fondly referred to as the LAGQ). His book Pumping Nylon has been a best-seller since it was first published in 1995, and is considered to be the ultimate guide to advanced guitar technique. When he is not concertizing or teaching master classes and workshops, Mr. Tennant lives in the Los Angeles area and is on the faculty of the University of Southern California's Thornton School of Music.

Etude

This piece by Carcassi is one of the best places to start developing your tremolo. Though its final tempo is considerably slower than a "real" tremolo, the skills you need are developed throughout this piece.

Practice Notes

1. Pay attention to your contact points and tone as you work through this etude, which utilizes both tremolo and arpeggio techniques.

2. Measures 1, 5, 9, and others like them use the standard tremolo format: *p-a-m-i*, with *p* playing the bass line and *a-m-i* playing the notes in the upper voice.

Track 34 *Etude*

Matteo Carcassi

Technical Supplements

The technical exercises in this book are intended to be starting points, not a strict regimen you must practice every day. Take these exercises (and those in other chapters) and create variations on them to expand their benefits and keep the process interesting. For example, below you'll find exercises for practicing artificial harmonics, which are by no means comprehensive—but, rather, they provide ideas for different ways you could practice.

Practice Notes

1. The first exercise is a chromatic scale on one string. You don't have to worry about string crossing, but you do have to reposition the right hand vertically on the fretboard for every note. To expand on that, you could do chromatic scales that cross strings, which would require both types of adjustment (vertical and horizontal) and provide further challenge.

2. The second exercise crosses strings but stays on one fret. You could practice the same exercise on different frets for a change of pace.

3. The third exercise alternates frets in a pattern (1st–3rd–1st–3rd). There are several other patterns you could substitute (for example: 1st–4th–1st–4th) using the same principle.

4. The fourth exercise adds a tremolo drone to a scale. You can do this with any scale, or turn the scale itself into the tremolo. Remember, these exercises are just starting points!

Exercises for Artificial Harmonics

A Minor Scale with Tremolo

Chapter 13: Musical Considerations

We've talked extensively about technique in this book but not much about musicianship. In all styles of music, *how* you play is as important as getting the notes right. I believe that this is rarely more noticeable than in playing the classical guitar, an instrument full of possibilities and subtleties. Failure to take advantage of these qualities is not only a missed opportunity but, ultimately, a failure to do justice to the music. This results in a less than interesting performance, which is certainly not the goal! There are a variety of musical tools you can use to bring out the intentions of the composer and the feel of the music.

Dynamics

The first place to start in creating a sense of expression with your music is by exploring the dynamic range of the instrument. Including those you've already learned, here are the basic dynamic markings and their meanings:

p	=	*piano*	=	soft
f	=	*forte*	=	loud
mp	=	*mezzo piano*	=	moderately soft
mf	=	*mezzo forte*	=	moderately loud
pp	=	*pianissimo*	=	very soft
ppp	=	*pianississimo*	=	very, very soft
ff	=	*fortissimo*	=	very loud
fff	=	*fortississimo*	=	very, very loud
sf	=	*sforzando*	=	a sudden strong accent
————	=	*crescendo*	=	gradually get louder
————	=	*decrescendo*	=	gradually get softer

Contemporary composers tend to include more markings in their music, while older compositions often have significantly fewer dynamic indications, or even none at all. The absence of indications does not excuse you from playing musically. The job of a performer is to bring the music to life, and that includes your interpretation of the dynamics, whether they are notated or not.

It is one thing to understand the markings and their meanings; it is entirely another thing to be able to execute these markings within the context of a composition. Playing with dynamics has an aesthetic, musical goal, but the execution is entirely technical. If you have not given any thought to how you would grow in volume from *piano* to *forte,* then, likely, you won't be able to do it with any sense of control when called upon in a piece. You must practice changing dynamic levels on open strings, in your scales, and in very familiar passages.

Practice Ideas

1. Try a phrase entirely *piano*, and be sure that no notes are popping out.

2. Try the same phrase *forte*, making sure that no notes are dipping under and that you are maintaining a great quality of sound.

3. Then, try the same phrase starting *piano* and ending *forte.*

4. Play the same phrase starting *forte* and ending *piano.*

5. Play the same phrase starting and ending *piano*, with a rise and fall in the middle.

As you move through different dynamic levels, listen carefully to be sure you are playing at the level you intend—not whatever dynamic level your fingers default to.

Tonal Colors

One of our more unique gifts on the classical guitar is the wide range of colors we can choose from to create our sound. The term "colors," in this sense, refers to the quality of sound, which can be varied by plucking the strings in different places.

Normal

As covered on page 19, the standard "normal" sound is produced when plucking near the bottom of the soundhole.

Ponticello

From the normal position, the closer you move your right hand toward the bridge, the *brighter* the sound becomes. This technique is referred to as *ponticello*, and it creates an interesting tonal character that can be a great asset in interpreting music.

Tasto

From the normal position, the closer you move your right hand toward the fingerboard, the warmer and richer the sound becomes. This is called *tasto*, or *dolce*.

You'll see the above terms written occasionally in the music. However, quite often, changing colors is something you will do without indication from the composer, based on your instincts of what character you'd like to bring out in the piece.

As with the execution of dynamics, the execution of different colors begins as a technical consideration. To move from normal to ponticello, the arm must slide to the right on the guitar; and to move from normal to tasto, the arm must slide to the left on the guitar. Your arm cannot be locked in position or this won't work! So, to achieve different colors, you must practice—again, outside the context of repertoire—the mechanics of changing the position of your right arm. These movements are small, but without some experience, your arm can feel disoriented.

Practice Ideas

1. Choose a scale and practice moving from normal to ponticello.

2. Using the same scale, practice moving from normal to tasto.

In repertoire, you will often want to change color at a section break. This makes it a bit easier to reset the right arm. But be sure to do your homework so that you can move seamlessly as the music demands.

Rubato

Rubato is the "give and take" of time in music, or playing with a flexible tempo for expressive purposes. Having a good pulse is critical, but so is knowing when a phrase needs to breathe a bit.

One of the best places to start experimenting with rubato is at the ends of phrases. In many pieces, you'll see the abbreviation *ritard.* or *rit.* (short for *ritardando*; also known as *rallentando*, abbreviated *rall.*) written at the end of a phrase. This is an indication to slow down to the end of that phrase. Think of how you pull your car into the driveway. You don't do it at 30 mph and slam on the brakes—you slow down and stop gradually. This sense of timing works well for many phrase endings, and that kind of common sense applies to phrasing in general.

Base your rubato on the demands of the phrase. This ability will come from experience and lots of listening. As with dynamic indications, the absence of the "rit." notation at the end of a phrase doesn't mean you can't or shouldn't slow down. Use your musical instincts.

Articulations

An *articulation* is the manner in which a note is performed, usually *legato* (smooth, connected) or *staccato* (short, detached). Articulation markings will sometimes appear in the music, but even if they don't, a musician is called upon to use their instincts to apply these articulations in an effective and aesthetically pleasing way.

Staccato is indicated with a dot above or below the notehead.

Check out the example below.

When staccato is indicated, there should be a slight separation between each note and it should sound like this:

Below is the same phrase with tenuto marks above each note to indicate a legato feel. Tenuto directs us to hold the notes for their full value, or even a little longer.

Remember, legato can also be indicated with a phrase marking, as in the example below.

Generally speaking, unless otherwise marked, most notes should be played legato. The indication by the composer just emphasizes that legato is a particularly important feature of the passage.

Vibrato

Vibrato is the slight altering of a pitch—up and down—by movement of the left hand. In other styles of guitar playing, one type of vibrato is produced by pulling a string toward the floor then back toward the ceiling in a repetitive motion. However, that technique is rarely used in classical guitar. The type of vibrato most used in classical guitar resembles the technique used by violinists. The string is pulled back and forth in the direction of the nut to the bridge. You can practice this motion on any single note (don't try with chords yet—that's much harder!), though it is best to start up around the 7th fret—it's easier to hear the results higher up on the fingerboard. The tip of the finger remains in place on the string, and you push and pull the string to alter the pitch. The left forearm rocks back and forth from the elbow joint to accommodate the motion. Watch some advanced players and study the motion, or, even better, consult with your private teacher. Using vibrato can be a bit tricky, but it's great to start experimenting with the concept, so you're ready to apply it when the right time arises.

Using Your New Musical Tools

Now that you know a bit more about how to make a piece interesting, it's your challenge to put your skills to work. Music is not a science, and there is no "right" way to play a piece. There are ways that work better than others, but often, there are many approaches that can make a piece sound great. You can be sure it *won't* sound great if you don't apply any musical ideas—just being "note perfect" does not make a good performance. So be sure to incorporate dynamics from the start when learning a piece. You may change your ideas as you go, but you'll be learning good habits of musical thinking.

The pieces that follow are more challenging than what we've seen so far in the book. If they are too challenging for you at this point, go back to some of the previous pieces and apply the musical elements we've been discussing in this chapter. Come back to the repertoire here when you're ready for a slightly bigger challenge. With all these pieces, remember to learn them bit by bit. Don't try to take on the entire composition in one sitting; learn phrase by phrase, with lots of quality repetition.

The following pieces provide many opportunities to put your newly discovered skills in dynamics and colors to use. Let the markings on the page serve as a launching pad for your creativity, and experiment with different ideas to bring the music to life.

Barcarolle

A *barcarolle* is a song that originates from the singing of gondoliers in Venice, Italy.

Practice Notes

1. This piece should have a gentle rocking feel, as you'd feel if in a gondola. Having an idea of what a piece is about can greatly help you with your interpretation. Knowing that this form originated as a kind of gentle folk music will guide your ideas regarding dynamics, tempo, and articulation.

2. Note the harmonics in measures 34–38, 58, and 62–64. All of these should be executed as artificial harmonics (both fingering and plucking the string with the right hand), even the notes that can be played as natural harmonics. The reason for this is that your left-hand fingers are forming chords that should not be disrupted by moving to another position.

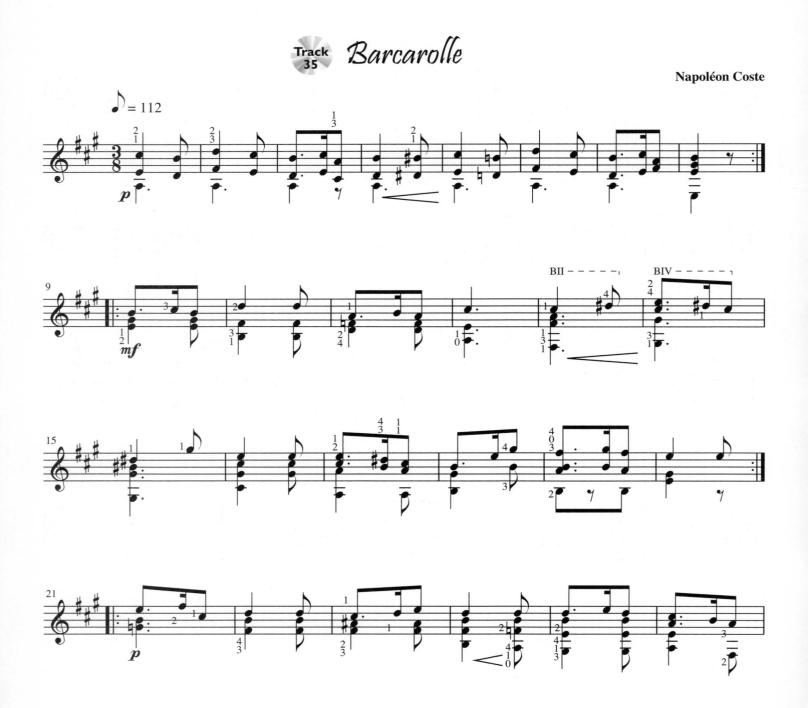

Track 35 Barcarolle

Napoléon Coste

La Paloma

This next piece, by Sebastián Yradier (1809–1865), is a *habanera*, which is a slow Cuban dance in *duple* time (meters with two beats, or pulses, per measure). This composition invites you to try out some of your new skills by experimenting with articulations.

Practice Notes

1. The bass has a recurring rhythmic pattern, which is typical of habaneras. If you aren't already familiar with how this type of piece typically sounds, do some research—listen to other habaneras and pay attention to how the bass is articulated; then, experiment with how you'd like to apply those ideas here.

2. This piece uses *drop D tuning,* where the 6th string (E) is tuned down to D (⑥ = D). For "La Paloma," you will only be playing the open 6th string—you won't have to fret any notes on this re-tuned string. (Note: Normally, it takes about three turns of the tuning peg to get from E to D. However, try going down nine turns, and then back up six. This helps the string adjust more quickly to the new pitch and gives you a chance at making it through the entire song in tune.)

La Paloma

Sebastián Yradier
arr. Francisco Tárrega

Divertissement in C

This piece is entirely without fingering indications. When played primarily in 1st position, most of the fingerings should be obvious.

Practice Notes

1. Be sure to write in any fingerings that are not immediately obvious to you—you'll learn the piece faster that way. Also, considering your options and marking in your choices will help you decide on smarter fingerings.

Track 37

Divertissement in C

Mauro Giuliani

Divertissement in F

Giuliani wrote many works suitable for the developing
guitarist. Here is another beautiful piece that embodies
the spirit of classical music.

Divertissement in F

Mauro Giuliani

Nocturne

The simple melody of "Nocturne" by Mertz is beautifully supported by the triplet accompaniment, and both voices will need musical attention to make this piece soar.

Practice Notes

1. No right-hand fingerings are given here, as you should find what works best for your hand in this piece, but be mindful to include natural arpeggio fingerings whenever possible.

2. The melody is in the top voice until the last three lines, at which point you should shift the melodic attention to the bass.

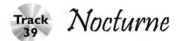

Johann Kaspar Mertz

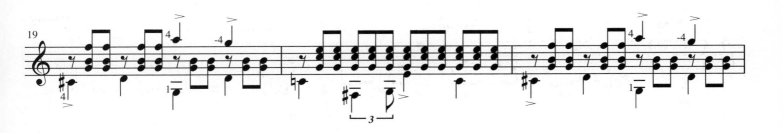

Two Pieces by Tárrega

It is unfathomable to have a book introducing the classical guitar without the inclusion of the following famous tunes by the great Spanish composer Francisco Tárrega. Both pieces are short, but not without their challenges.

Maneuver carefully through the many shifts and never lose sight of the soaring melodies that have made these songs staples of classical guitar repertoire.

Track 40 *Lágrima*

Francisco Tárrega

Adelita

Track 41

Francisco Tárrega

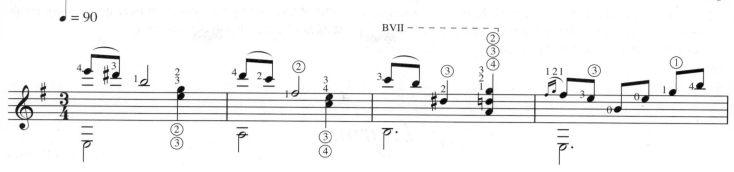

Vals

Now, let's learn a waltz by Tárrega. This piece provides a few more challenges, including quicker shifts, ornaments, and capturing the spirit of the waltz.

Practice Notes

1. This is a faster-paced work, so proceed slowly and carefully to avoid developing bad habits, especially with the left hand.

2. "Vals" is in drop D tuning, so don't forget to drop your low-E string to D.

3. Notice that this piece has three voices. The lower and middle voices have stems facing downward and the upper voice has stems facing upward. Each voice has its own identity: the upper voice contains the melody, the lower voice consists of bass notes, and the middle voice is made up of other accompanying chord tones. The three parts combine to produce a strong waltz rhythm.

4. At the end of the piece, you will see the indication *D.C. al Coda*. This tells you to go back to the beginning and play to the "To Coda" marking, then skip down to the Coda (⊕). Do not take the repeats the second time through the piece.

Track 42 *Vals*

Francisco Tárrega

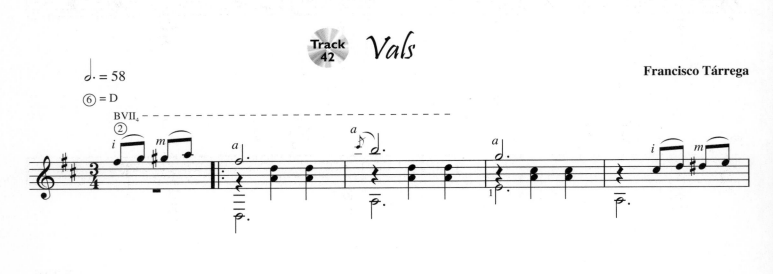

Malagueña

"Malagueña" is the longest (and final) piece in this book, though not necessarily the hardest.

Practice Notes

1. Don't feel obliged to learn the entire piece at once, or even at all. There are several points at which you could create an ending to this piece, making it a shorter performance requiring less study time. For example, any of the sections that are set off by double bars could be eliminated entirely. All of the sections begin and end in E, so it's not a problem to make a few cuts to adapt the piece to your current technical capabilities.

2. As always, take your time—especially with the trickier parts.

Track 43 *Malagueña*

Francisco Tárrega

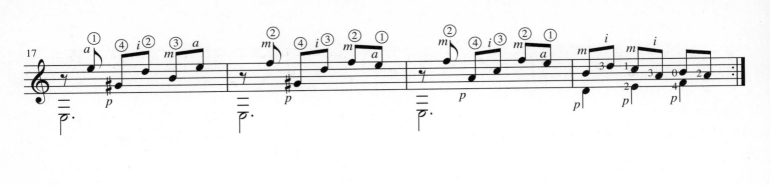

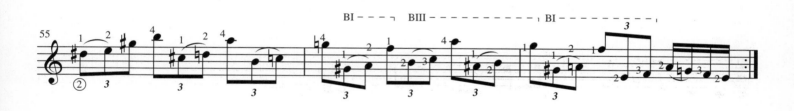

Continuing Your Growth as a Classical Guitarist

Congratulations! By working through this book, you've gained a lot of ground in your technical abilities. As you go forth and seek other pieces to expand your repertoire, revisit on a regular basis the fundamentals presented here, along with the basic technical exercises. Of course, we all want to learn new pieces—but without good technique, everything is much harder than it needs to be. Make sure that you're maintaining control of your hands, using good positions, and always getting a great tone.

Also, seek out a good teacher in your area—there is no substitute for outside perspective and experience.

Listen to recordings and attend live performances of classical guitar music. By listening and watching, you will gain a greater understanding of dynamics, expression, interpretation, repertoire, and much more.

Good luck, and enjoy your discovery of the world of classical guitar.

3D WORLD

OCEAN

Paul Harrison

Capella

A WORLD OF WATER

Over 70 per cent of our planet's surface is covered in water and the majority of it is seawater. Most of this water can be divided into five large areas called oceans even though, in reality, all of the oceans are joined together.

THE BIGGEST

The largest ocean in the world is the Pacific, which is almost as big as all the other oceans put together. The Pacific is also the world's deepest ocean and is home to many huge undersea mountains and deep trenches. The deepest part of the Pacific is called the Challenger Deep in the Mariana Trench which is an amazing 11 kilometres/7 miles below the surface of the waves!

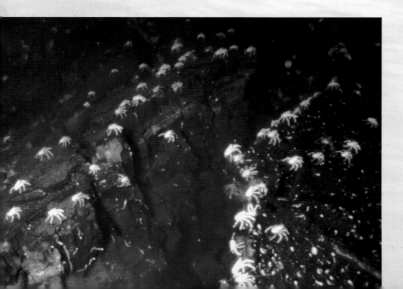

IN THE MIDDLE

The Indian Ocean is the body of water between the east coast of Africa and Australia. It is the third largest ocean and holds about a fifth of all the oceans' water.

The oceans account for around 97 per cent of all the earth's water.

THE SMALLEST

The smallest of the world's oceans is the Arctic, which is the area of water around the North Pole. Much of the Arctic Ocean is covered in ice, either packed together around the Pole or floating about as icebergs.

BUSY SEAS

The second largest ocean is also one of the busiest. As the Atlantic Ocean separates the USA from Europe, there is a great deal of sea traffic which crosses the water between these continents.

NEW ONE

In 2000, scientists named a new ocean, the Southern Ocean. It had always been there of course, but in the past it had been included as part of the other oceans. Scientists realised that the area of water around Antarctica had its own unique traits, so it was agreed that it should form its own, distinct ocean. It is now the fourth largest of the oceans.

WATERY WONDERLAND

The oceans are teeming with life from the microscopic to the massive. As with life on land, most sea life relies on sunlight to survive, so most living things in the sea live in the zone where sunlight can penetrate the surface.

SMALL BUT IMPORTANT

Plankton is the general name for the tiny creatures and plants that drift about in the sunlit zone of the ocean. There are billions of them – which is just as well as they are at the bottom of the food chain.

ALL SORTS

Not all the animals that depend on the sea to survive actually live in the water full-time. Mammals such as seals and sea lions and reptiles such as marine iguanas stay on land to sleep and breed, only going to the oceans to hunt for food. Then there are sea birds – hundreds of different species that also rely on the oceans to survive. Most sea birds, such as puffins, seagulls and pelicans either dive into the water to catch fish or skim across the surface for them. Penguins are expert swimmers, having lost the ability to fly but having gained flipper-like wings instead.

ALL KINDS OF LIFE

The upper layers of the ocean are home to a staggering range of animal life. Obviously there are fish – thousands of different species from huge whale sharks to colourful tropical fish – but there are also jellyfish, snails, corals, anemones and mammals such as dolphins, whales and the rare manatee. Then there are reptiles too, such as sea snakes and seven different types of turtle.

Most people think seaweed is a plant, but scientists call it algae. True plants have roots, leaves, seeds or flowers – seaweed doesn't.

WEEDY WONDERS

The sunlit zone is the only part of the ocean that supports plant life and seaweed. One type of seaweed is called kelp and it can grow in large groups, called forests. Kelp forests are home to many types of sea creature including seahorses. The dense seaweed provides plenty of places for these smaller creatures to hide and escape from predators.

INTO THE DARKNESS

The bottom of the ocean, where sunlight cannot penetrate, is a very different world from the teeming waters above. Here it is dark and cold. There is little oxygen in the water for animals to breathe and the pressure from the weight of the water above is enormous. Yet this forbidding place is home to a surprising array of ocean life.

DEEP DIVING

Some creatures, such as the sperm whale, are only visitors to the dark zones of the oceans. Scientists do not know exactly how deep a sperm whale can dive but some think that it could be over 2 kilometres/1.3 miles. One of the sperm whale's favourite foods is the giant squid, but how the whales can find them – or any other food – in the dark water is something of a mystery.

Sunken ships take a long time to rust in the deepest parts of the ocean because there is so little oxygen.

BIG MOUTH

One of the strangest looking sea creatures is the gulper eel. At nearly 2 metres/6 feet long the eel is little more than a large mouth, stomach and thin tail. As its name suggests, the gulper eel likes to eat and is not fussy about what it munches on. Large meals aren't a problem – the eel simply unhinges its jaw to make its mouth even bigger!

BRIGHT LIGHT

Many deep sea fish can generate their own light and, for species such as the angler fish, this light can be a useful aid for hunting its prey. Female angler fish have what looks like a rod sticking out above their mouths. At the end of the rod is a piece of flesh that glows. This attracts small fish, which the angler fish quickly snaps up in its toothy jaws.

IN HOT WATER

Not everywhere at the bottom of the ocean is cold. When cracks appear in the earth's crust, cold water comes into contact with magma – molten rock that can be as hot as 1000°C/1832°F. The hot water is forced away from the crack, creating a watery volcano. This is called a deep sea vent and many species of fish, shrimp, crab and octopus have adapted to live in these super-warm conditions.

PEOPLE AND THE SEA

People have made their living from the oceans for thousands of years. However, the world's seas can be unpredictable places to work, so a job on the oceans always carries a risk of injury — or even death.

TRAWLING THE OCEANS

One of the oldest jobs associated with the sea is that of fishermen. Today, fishing boats catch over 90 million tonnes/198 million pounds of fish each year. The fish are caught by boats called trawlers, though these boats can be very different in size and in the way they are used. Many are equipped with onboard freezing equipment which means the boats can stay at sea for weeks at a time. Sometimes large factory ships are used. These boats process the catch from many different trawlers and have huge freezer compartments for storing the fish.

ISOLATION

One of the most isolated places a person can work is on an oil platform in the middle of the ocean, drilling for oil on the sea bed. As these platforms are often many miles from shore, the workers stay there for two weeks at a time. The platforms have to be self-sufficient too, in case bad weather means that help cannot come in the event of an emergency. Each platform has its own doctor and even a mini hospital.

BIG SHIPS

There are two different types of navy: the merchant navy, which consists of civilian ships carrying trade goods; and the military navy, which is part of a country's armed forces. The biggest armed ships are the aircraft carriers which are over 330 metres/1080 feet long and carry a crew of more than 5,500 sailors.

Nuclear submarines never run out of fuel, so the only reason they need to come to the surface is to take on more provisions.

FUN ON THE WAVES

Not all human activity on the waves is hard work, of course. Watersports are always popular, be it surfing, sailing, or just going for a swim. Offshore powerboating is one of the world's most expensive and fastest sports. These high-performance vessels can reach speed in excess of 160 kilometres/100 miles per hour — a phenomenal speed over water.

HUMAN EXPLORATION

As water covers so much of the planet, it was only a matter of time before humans felt the need to explore it. We are still exploring the oceans to this day and are yet to uncover all of its secrets.

FLAT EARTH

It is thought people used to believe that the world was flat because of the straight edge seen on the horizon across the oceans. However, sailors knew this wasn't the case. They had always known that there was a curve to the earth as they had seen the way a boat could disappear over the horizon and then return safe and sound.

LOOKING UNDERWATER

Exploring what lies beneath the waves has always been fascinating to people. Of course the biggest problem with underwater exploration is breathing underwater. As early as the 4th century BC the ancient Greeks had developed a kind of diving bell. This was an upturned container big enough for divers to stick their heads into to get a lungful of air before continuing with their work. The first diving helmet, complete with oxygen supply, was designed centuries later in 1829. It was based on the traditional knight-in-armour helmet.

GOING DOWN

To have a good look around at the bottom of the sea, explorers and scientists use a machine called a bathyscaphe. These are like submarines, but are constructed to survive the water pressure at extreme depths. In 1960 a bathyscaphe called *Trieste* even made it to the bottom of the Mariana Trench, the deepest point on earth.

The wreck of the *Titanic* will be completely destroyed in the next 50 years if it remains a tourist attraction.

TRADERS AND EXPLORERS

Historically, the first explorers of the oceans were seafaring traders and fishermen. Ancient civilizations such as the Phoenicians were always pushing back the boundaries of the known world as they travelled further and further to find new places to sell their wares. Many people believe that Basque fishermen from Spain and France were the first to cross the Atlantic to America as they searched for fish.

DANGEROUS WATERS

As any sailor could tell you, the oceans can be dangerous places. A boat hundreds of kilometres from shore can fall victim to a variety of unpleasant forces of nature.

OCEAN TWISTER

Tornadoes are deadly spirals of wind that can occur over land; waterspouts are their oceanic relatives. Waterspout winds can reach over 200 kilometres/ 125 miles per hour and, like their land-based equivalents, can cause terrible damage mainly due to flying debris. What's more, if you see one waterspout you'll probably see another one as they generally appear in groups.

SPINNING AROUND

If you have ever watched how the water drains from a sink or bath then you've got a good idea of what a whirlpool looks like. Whirlpools can occur in the oceans and are generally the result of tidal activity. Although whirlpools can be as much as 75 metres/245 feet across, they are not strong enough to pull a boat into its swirling vortex. However, you would be ill-advised to swim near a whirlpool as they are more than capable of drowning a person.

FREAK WAVES

Every so often an especially large wave will surge across the oceans. No one is entirely sure why these rogue waves occur and hundreds of ships are believed to have been sunk by them. The waves can reach over 30 metres/98 feet and can affect even the biggest ships. In 1978 the cargo ship *München* was sunk by a freak wave and everyone on board was drowned.

One ship is lost every week on the world's oceans.

FLOATING MOUNTAINS

Icebergs are huge lumps of frozen fresh water that have broken off from glaciers and are floating free in the oceans. As the sinking of the *Titanic* proved, hitting an iceberg can have disastrous consequences. This is why there are now regular ice-spotting patrols in the Atlantic Ocean to warn ships of imminent problems.

MYTHS AND LEGENDS

Throughout history, ships and boats have disappeared without a trace. There are good scientific explanations for these sudden disappearances, but in earlier unenlightened times strange stories circulated about what sailors could find in the oceans.

SOMETHING FISHY

Sightings of sea serpents are as old as the hills, but there is one sea monster for which there is good scientific evidence. The oar fish is about 9 metres/30 feet long and looks exactly as you would imagine a sea serpent to look. There are also snakes that live in the oceans, so these may have added to the myth as well.

FATAL SINGING

Mermaids were meant to be half woman, half fish. In some stories mermaids would lure sailors to their doom on jagged rocks with their beautiful voices. The most likely explanation was that sailors had spotted either seals or manatees in the water and had mistaken them for people. However, neither are particularly good singers.

Islands can rise from the ocean! The peaks of undersea volcanoes can emerge gradually over a number of years, forming small islands.

MISSING CITY

Plato, the ancient Greek writer, recorded the fate of Atlantis – an island in the Atlantic that disappeared into the sea. No one has ever found any proof that such an island ever existed but that has not stopped people speculating as to where it may have been. To ancient mariners wary of towering waves and violent storms, the idea of an island falling into the sea probably felt like an all too real possibility.

TENTACLE TERROR

Tales of ships attacked by a huge octopus-like creature date back hundreds of years. It is quite possible that these stories may be based on sightings of a giant squid, an animal that is known to fight with sperm whales.

This edition published in 2008 by Arcturus Publishing Limited
26/27 Bickels Yard, 151–153 Bermondsey Street,
London SE1 3HA

Author: Paul Harrison
Editor: Fiona Tulloch
Designers: Emily Gibson and Mike Reynolds

Picture credits:
AKG: page 14, right.
Art Archive: page 10, right.
Corbis: front cover (background); title page, top left, centre and
far right; page 2, right; page 4, left; page 6, right; page 7; page 8,
left; page 10.
FLPA: page 6, left.
Getty: front cover (shark); page 3; page 9; page 14, centre.
Kobal Collection: page 15.

NHPA: page 14, left.
Nature Picture Library: page 6, centre.
Science Photo Library: title page, bottom left; page 2, left and
centre; page 5; page 8, centre; page 10, left; page 12, left; page 16.

3D images by Pinsharp 3D Graphics

Printed in China

ISBN: 978-1-84193-884-4